Treating
Alcohol Problems

Wiley Series on Treating Addiction

Series editors, Robert Holman Coombs and William A. Howatt

TREATING DRUG PROBLEMS
Arthur W. Blume

TREATING ALCOHOL PROBLEMS
Frederick Rotgers
Beth Arburn Davis

TREATING GAMBLING PROBLEMS
William G. McCown

Treating
Alcohol Problems

Frederick Rotgers

Beth Arburn Davis

WILEY

John Wiley & Sons, Inc.

Copyright © 2006 by John Wiley & Sons, Inc. All rights reserved.

Published by John Wiley & Sons, Inc., Hoboken, New Jersey.
Published simultaneously in Canada.

Library of Congress Cataloging-in-Publication Data:
    Rotgers, Frederick.
      Treating alcohol problems / by Frederick Rotgers, Beth Arburn
    Davis.
        p. cm. -- (Wiley series on treating addiction)
      ISBN-13: 978-0-471-49432-4 (pbk.)
      ISBN-10: 0-471-49432-1 (pbk.)
      1. Alcoholism--Treatment.   I. Davis, Beth Arburn. II. Title.
    III. Series.
      [DNLM: 1. Alcoholism--therapy. 2. Alcoholism--diagnosis.
    3. Patient Care Planning.   WM 274 R844t 2006]
    RC565.R573 2006
    616.86'106--dc22

                                    2005022393

Printed in the United States of America.

10 9 8 7 6 5 4 3 2 1

We dedicate this book to our spouses, Jo and Gerry, and to Beth Davis's father Will Arburn, her son Justin, and her grandson Hunter. Thanks for all your love and support.

CONTENTS

Chapter 2: Identifying Alcohol Problems: "I Know It When I See It! Or Do I?"

Chapter 3: Finding and Getting the Best Out of Professional Resources

Chapter 4: Assessment and Treatment Planning

Chapter 5: Treatment Tools, Programs, and Theories: Helping Clients Overcome Problem Drinking

Chapter 6: When and How Should Clients Be Discharged to Aftercare?

Chapter 7: How to Increase Recovery Success, Minimize "Slips," and Avoid Chronic Relapse

Chapter 8: Culture, Coaching, and Change: Moving Beyond Alcohol Problems

SERIES PREFACE

Most books on addiction are written for only 10% of those who deal with addicted people—typically, for experts who specialize in addiction. By contrast, we designed the Wiley Series on Treating Addictions primarily for the other 90%—the many health service providers and family members who, though not addictionologists, regularly deal with those who suffer from various addictive disorders.

All volumes in this series define addiction as "an attachment to, or dependence upon, any substance, thing, person or idea so single-minded and intense that virtually all other realities are ignored or given second place—and consequences, even lethal ones, are disregarded" (Mack, 2000).

Considering that over one's lifetime more than one fourth (27%) of the entire population will suffer from a substance abuse problem (Kessler et al., 1994), many family members and all human services providers will, sooner or later, be confronted with these problems. Unfortunately, few have received any training to prepare them for this challenging task.

Legal and illegal (minors) alcohol consumption continues to be a serious concern in North America. Alcohol-related motor vehicle accidents kill someone very 31 minutes and non-fatality accidents injure someone every two minutes (National Highway Traffic Safety Administration, 2004). The United States Department of Health and Human Services (2005) reports on its website that a 1993 study showed that domestic violence was 15 times higher in households where husbands were described as often drunk, as opposed to never drunk. The United States Department of Justice (2005) reports on its website that in 2002 nearly one million violent crimes occurred in which victims perceived the victim to have been drinking at the time of the offense. This drug continues to cost billions of dollars in damage and thousands of lives each year in North America.

We are convinced that you will find the work of Fred Rotgers and Beth Davis to be a practical and comprehensive book about treating alcohol problems. Both authors have impressive academic backgrounds as well as proven track records in treating alcohol substance disorders.

Their book will serve as an excellent primer and helpful resource for everyone—including experts on this subject—who want to gain a clearer understanding about the social and psychological dynamics of this problem and what one can do to help addicted clients and associates.

We predict that you will find this book to be an invaluable practical resource.

Robert Holman Coombs, PhD
William A. Howatt, PhD
Series Editors

Robert Holman Coombs passed away while this book was being prepared. We are indebted to his contributions to this and other books in this series.

PREFACE

This is a book about helping people overcome problems associated with drinking alcohol. We have designed the book first and foremost as a guide for general clinicians who are not necessarily going to be providing primary treatment for alcohol problems, but who want to understand how best to work with their patients whose drinking creates problems. This book is also intended for alcohol treatment specialists who are searching for a new, evidence-based approach to working with problem drinkers, both those who suffer from diagnosable alcohol problems (alcohol abuse or dependence) and those who have problems associated with drinking but don't yet meet diagnostic criteria for an alcohol use disorder.

We have not attempted to produce a comprehensive textbook on alcohol and alcohol problems, largely because we believe that clinicians are unlikely to find much of what would be included in such a volume directly useful helping clients. We have, however, presented a broad overview of evidence-based approaches, a summary of an approach that we believe makes sense given the available evidence, and a suggested list of readings and resources that clinicians can access should they desire to explore the issues we summarize in more detail.

Many experienced alcohol treatment clinicians will find this book disturbing. We believe that this disturbance will likely stem from belief in the numerous myths about alcohol and alcohol problems that have developed over the decades of the latter 20th century and often been uncritically accepted by clinicians and clinical training programs in the United States. These myths have come to color how most people, even clinicians who disavow them on a conscious level, view these problems and the people who suffer from them. At the beginning of each chapter of this book we ask questions designed to evoke these myths, and then present arguments and data that we believe debunk most of them.

Alcohol treatment had its origins in the United States in the early 19th century. Before that time there was no notion of "alcoholism" (that term was first used by a Swedish physician, Magnus Huss to describe patients whose drinking created problems in their lives), although as early as the beginning of the 19th century, Philadelphia physician and signer of the Declaration of Independence, Benjamin Rush wrote about the development and consequences of problematic drinking. In his "Moral Thermometer," Rush delineated what he believed was an inevitable downward spiral of problems associated with alcohol, leading eventually to incarceration and death for those who did not reform their drinking or stop altogether.

Since Rush, there have been many approaches proposed to help people with alcohol problems (see William White's wonderful book *Slaying the Dragon: A History of Addictions Treatment in America* for a comprehensive and highly readable account of the development of treatment in the United States). The dominant approach (used, according to a survey conducted by the National Institute on Drug Abuse in the 1990s, by more than 90% of treatment programs in the United States) is one loosely derived from the principles of Alcoholics Anonymous (AA). Alcohol treatment in the United States is intimately entwined with AA, although treatment practices are not always consistent with the AA philosophy as originally proposed by Bill Wilson, AA's co-founder and the author of the AA handbook, *Alcoholics Anonymous*, also known as "The Big Book" (TBB).

The approach to helping people with alcohol problems change, as described in TBB, is a program of attraction. Bill Wilson explicitly disavows harsh confrontation and coercion in his approach and indicates that a program of attraction rather than prescription worked best in helping people initially affiliate with AA during the organization's early years. TBB also explicitly recognizes that not every person with alcohol-related problems is an "alcoholic," and it acknowledges that there are non-abstinence outcomes that resolve alcohol-related problems for at least some people. Finally, TBB relies on a process of self-identification with the people whose stories form the second half of the book as the primary mechanism by which people with alcohol problems affiliate with AA. The process is one of hearing (at AA meetings) and reading (in TBB and other AA literature) about the accounts of others, finding themes and subjects that resonate with the problem drinker's own experience, and deciding for oneself that the approach represented by AA is the one that will most likely be productive "for me."

In contrast to this highly patient-focused, empathetic, and non-confrontational approach that recognizes a variety of possible resolutions to alcohol problems, the treatment system in the United States has, until very recently, been none of these. In fact, the treatment system in the United States, despite a heavy reliance on the so-called "disease" model of alcohol problems, has tended to be highly program-focused, non-empathetic (in the sense that the patient's views are often discounted as reflecting either pathological denial or the "disease" itself), and work with patients is frequently highly confrontational, often aggressively so. Patients are told that they *must* engage in a variety of activities, most putatively associated with AA (although as we shall see later, these are either not part of AA or directly antithetical to AA principles!), and are also told that there is but a single, viable resolution to *all* alcohol problems—lifelong abstinence—often accompanied by lifelong attendance at AA meetings. In fact, treatment providers who claim to be proponents of AA and the 12-step approaches, often recommend a highly confrontational and coercive approach for families and other concerned significant others (CSOs) to use in helping motivate the problem drinker to enter treatment. This approach, called "intervention," presumably aims at "raising the bottom" for the problem drinker (this tactic is loosely based on the AA notion that alcoholics will only think of seeking help when their lives have become unmanageable—or, in more colloquial terms, when they have "hit bottom") by a total immersion in a confrontational encounter with his/her CSOs who are taught how to recite a litany of harms done by the patient to them and to others. The patient is then, in the best outcome of the intervention, whisked off to a treatment program. For us, a careful reading of the seminal 12-step thinking upon which most U.S. treatment is putatively based suggests that a treatment process that was genuinely based on the 12-steps and AA philosophy would look very different from the one currently in place.

Others have pointed out that our treatment system is a "one size fits all" system in which virtually every patient receives the same treatment, regardless of individual differences. Yet, research findings have argued against such a monolithic system for more than a decade (at least since the Institute of Medicine Report on *Broadening the Base of Treatment for Alcohol Problems,* published in 1990). Research also shows, quite conclusively, that the confrontational, prescriptive, abstinence-only approach not only is ineffective for many people who undergo such treatment, but (and this is perhaps most important) the lack of any other options for getting help for problems related to drinking, even when one is not an "alcoholic" (or qualified for an alcohol use disorder diagnosis according to the *DSM-IV-TR*), exerts a strong discouraging influence, keeping people from seeking treatment early on in the development of problems when those problems would be most amenable to change.

The current system also fails to take into account research that shows how people (1) become motivated to change and (2) actually change problem behavior. Research in recent years has shown over and over again that strong motivation for change requires a context in which (1) patient autonomy is recognized and supported and patient choices about courses of action are encouraged and not dismissed as the product of disease, (2) a relationship with helpers that is empathetic, understanding and respectful of the patient, and (3) skills training is provided for those who lack the basic skills to effect the changes they have decided upon.

These principles are not only consistent with those of AA as set forth in TBB, they are also highly consistent with contemporary biomedical ethics, which places a heavy emphasis on patient autonomy, informed consent, and absence of coercion in treatment. They are also consistent with a number of court decisions

handed down over the past two decades that have tended to see coerced attendance at 12-step programs as a violation of the Establishment Clause of the U.S.
Constitution. That clause ensures the free practice of religion, as well as freedom
from state coercion to engage in specific religious activities. Given AA's reliance
on protestant Christian theology for some of its philosophy, it is hardly surprising that coerced attendance at AA and other 12-step groups has been challenged
in the courts.

It is our belief that alcohol treatment needs to return to its philosophical roots
as presented by Bill Wilson in *Alcoholics Anonymous*. Not only is such a return
consistent with the direction that medicine and other healthcare professions have
moved in terms of ethical treatment of patients, it is supported by substantial scientific research carried out over the last 30 years or more. In this book, we present an approach to working with patients whose drinking has created problems
that we believe combines both philosophy and science in an approach that is not
only much more respectful of the patient as an autonomous human being than
has traditionally been the case, but which we believe is strongly supported by
research on the treatment of alcohol problems.

Much of what we will present in the pages that follow has been proposed,
implemented and studied under the rubric of "harm reduction." While we
believe in the basic principles of harm reduction, we also believe that the term
itself has been politicized, become polarizing, and has clouded the important
issues in working with problem drinkers. We prefer to call our approach an
"evidence-based, patient-centered" approach. In the chapters that follow we will
present that approach, along with discussion of the research supporting it.

This book is not for readers who already believe they know *the* best way to
work with problem drinkers. It is a book for readers who want to help patients
address drinking problems in a humane, respectful fashion that relies on science,
rather than personal experience and belief, to guide treatment. We believe the
time has come to bring to alcohol treatment broadly the fruits of decades of
research. We also think that frontline mental health practitioners are the ones to
do this. If you think so, too, then this book is for you.

CHAPTER 1

Conceptual Foundations: Defining Alcohol Problems

After reading this chapter, you will be able to answer true or false to the following statements:

1. Either you have an alcohol problem or you don't. True or False?
2. Most people who have problems with alcohol need treatment to overcome them. True or False?
3. Alcohol problems are mostly inherited. True or False?
4. Lifelong abstinence is the only way to recover from alcohol problems. True or False?

Answers on p. 21.

Alcohol Problems: What Are They, Who's Got Them, Who Hasn't, Who Might?

Alcohol is the most widely used drug in the United States after caffeine (we do love our Starbuck's). In fact, according to statistics compiled by the Centers for Disease Control (CDC), in 2001 nearly 63% of Americans over the age of 18 reported being a current drinker of alcohol. Compare this with about 23% of the adult population who smoke cigarettes and far fewer people who use illegal drugs. Yet alcohol is a drug about which society is extremely ambivalent, as the quotations at the beginning of this chapter surely demonstrate. While only about 7% of males and slightly less than 3% of females over the age of 18 suffer from "diagnosable" problems related to alcohol use, in 2001 nearly a third of all Americans surveyed reported that they drank five or more drinks (the level at which alcohol consumption begins to be associated reliably with negative consequences) on one occasion at least once during the past year. More startling is that 15% reported drinking at this level at least once a month, according to the CDC.

What do all these statistics and quotations mean? What they mean is that alcohol use is both a pleasant and important aspect of life for many Americans, and a source of difficulties for many others. The difficulties experienced by people who use alcohol include alcohol-related health problems, lost productivity at work, crime, motor vehicle crashes and other accidents. In 2000, the National Institute on Alcohol Abuse and Alcoholism estimated that the total monetary cost of these alcohol-related negative consequences would be more than $184 billion. That's "billion" with a "b"! That's nearly as much as the gross national product of Poland, and more than the gross national products of Indonesia and Thailand.

With alcohol consumption clearly bringing immense costs, it's important that we, as a society, begin to develop systematic ways of both preventing costs from occurring and reducing costs to individuals for whom they have already occurred. However, alcohol can also bring immense pleasure, and there are documented health benefits associated with moderate alcohol use. These benefits are such that the U.S. Department of Agriculture now includes a small amount of alcohol consumption in its daily guidelines for a healthy diet.

> "The sway of alcohol over mankind is unquestionably due to its power to stimulate the mystical faculties of human nature.... sobriety diminishes, discriminates and says 'no' drunkenness expands, unites, and says 'yes.'"
>
> —WILLIAM JAMES

The dilemma we face is in distinguishing alcohol use that is likely to cause harm, or already has done so, from alcohol use that is likely to bring with it benefits to subjective well being and health. To do so, we need to look beyond how much a particular individual drinks (quantity) to a variety of factors that are often overlooked by non-professionals in ascribing the label of "problem" to a person's drinking. These factors include, but are not limited to age, height, weight, ethnicity, gender, occupation (yes, your work does affect the likelihood that you will use alcohol in a problematic way), family environment, and other psychological and behavioral factors. As we consider various definitions we will see how these factors come into play, and how important it is to consider them in understanding and reacting to a particular person's drinking.

Defining Alcohol Problems

Before we can examine how we define alcohol problems, a few words about alcohol itself are in order.

Alcohol is a psychoactive drug. As such, it is a substance that many (in fact, most) drinkers use without problems. What makes people drink in the first place? As with any psychoactive substance, alcohol use is driven primarily by a desire to achieve a particular effect. The exact nature of that effect may vary from person to person, but desired changes in emotion, thought, and behavior are what motivates alcohol use for every drinker.

So, what are these effects? Well, it's important to recognize that alcohol does not affect all individuals in the same way, even at a biochemical level. Thus, many people of East Asian heritage (perhaps as many as one-third) respond to even small amounts of alcohol with an extremely unpleasant flushing reaction that makes alcohol consumption for these people an unpleasant experience. For most people, however, alcohol has a well-known pharmacological effect. Initially the effect is one of stimulation (seemingly contrary to alcohol's classification as a central nervous system depressant drug). However, as the drinker continues to consume alcohol and the percentage of alcohol in the blood and brain increases, alcohol's effects clearly become depressant. Motor and cognitive functioning begins to be altered first, and eventually, at high enough blood alcohol concentrations, respiratory arrest and death may occur.

Many of us have seen individuals who were intoxicated on alcohol. We've seen people who were unsteady on their feet, slurred their speech, had bloodshot eyes and flushed skin, were overly boisterous, or, to the contrary, fell asleep in the midst of a crowd of party-goers. We also may have seen drinkers who became hostile, depressed, happy. In addition to producing many of these effects, alcohol also affects reaction time and ability to rapidly process peripheral information. This is what makes driving a car under the influence of alcohol so risky. It's not that the drinker can't operate the car and keep it on the road adequately. It's that intoxicated drivers can't react quickly or effectively to sudden or unexpected changes (e.g., a car pulling out of a side street or a pedestrian walking in the road rather than on the sidewalk) and are more likely to crash as a result.

In problem drinkers, particularly those whose drinking is chronic and heavy and who have developed a high tolerance for alcohol's effects, many of these common signs of intoxication may not appear at all. One of us, for example, evaluated a client who, after more than a decade of heavy daily drinking, needed to maintain his blood alcohol concentration at .25% (the percentage of blood content that is alcohol, also often written as 250mg/deciliter) in order to forestall withdrawal symptoms. During the years prior to the evaluation, this client ran a business, was well liked by his customers and never had so much as a DUI arrest. He never appeared intoxicated to people around him who were unaware of his drinking, although he did always have thermos of vodka and orange juice handy in case his blood alcohol concentration dropped below comfortable levels. This client needed to drink simply in order to feel "normal" and to function. The behavioral signs of intoxication were largely invalid for him—he behaved "normally" when drunk!

Alcohol as a drug is somewhat different from other substances we think of as psychoactive drugs (e.g., marijuana, heroin, cocaine, methamphetamines). Alcohol is a very weak drug compared to other so-called recreational drugs. Effective doses of alcohol are measured in grams, while effective doses of other drugs are measured in milligrams. Nonetheless, alcohol is highly effective in altering mood and behavior largely because it readily crosses the blood-brain barrier. In fact, because it is soluble in water, alcohol diffuses throughout all bodily tissues.

While the exact mechanism through which alcohol exerts its psychoactive effects is not fully understood, it is clear that alcohol works through affecting neurochemistry in ways similar to other depressant or sedative drugs that alleviate anxiety. This can lead to the phenomenon of "cross tolerance" where individuals may find that they become more tolerant to the effects of alcohol when they are in the practice of using other sedative/hypnotic drugs, such as Valium or Xanax (though not at the same time that they are under the influence of alcohol).

> "Drunkenness is nothing but voluntary madness."
>
> —SENECA

As with other psychoactive drugs, pharmacology isn't the whole story of the drug's effects. Both psychological and environmental factors contribute to the effect alcohol has on a particular individual in a particular instance. Norman Zimberg, a Harvard psychiatrist, identified these three factors: drug (the pharmacological properties of a drug), set (the psychological and physiological factors unique to the particular individual), and setting (the context in which the substance is used) as being the multiple determinants of a drug's effects, especially at lower doses. All of these factors also come into play in the development of problems related to alcohol. The fact that alcohol effects are multi-factorial, rather than simply due to the pharmacology of alcohol itself, makes the whole issue of defining and identifying alcohol problems highly complicated.

Despite the complexity of alcohol problems, several proposed definitions are worth examining. These definitions vary in the extent to which they involve theoretical views of the nature of drinking problems (i.e., views that include thinking and concepts that grow out of popular and uncontrolled clinical studies of people with alcohol problems), but interestingly none focuses on alcohol use as a primary feature of alcohol problems. There are two types of definitions we will consider: Drinking Definitions and Diagnosis Definitions. Drinking Definitions describe aspects of drinking itself, while Diagnosis Definitions describe types of problems that arise from drinking. The Drinking Definitions we will discuss are: "harmful" drinking, "hazardous" drinking, "moderate" (or "controlled") drinking, and "binge" drinking. The Diagnosis Definitions we will review are the American Society of Addiction Medicine/American Medical Association definition of "alcoholism," and the American Psychiatric Association definitions of "Alcohol Abuse" and "Alcohol Dependence."

The various definitions of these terms serve to highlight controversies within the field that have often stood in the way of understanding drinking problems and developing effective ways of helping people overcome them. In fact, the same terms are often defined differently in different countries, which underscores the variability of both our views of drinking problems and the ways in which people are affected by alcohol consumption.

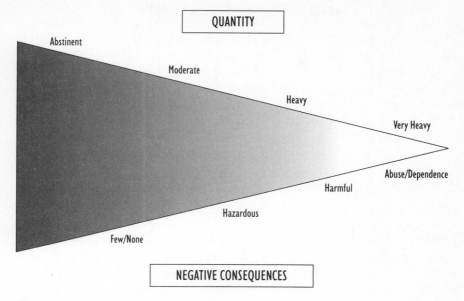

Figure 1.1: Continuum of alcohol problems.

Source: Adapted from the Institute of Medicine (1990).

Though we use what seem to be categorical terms to describe alcohol problems, it is important to recognize that these problems actually lie along a continuum, with no clear demarcation between the levels and types of problems. In 1990, the Institute of Medicine of the National Academy of Sciences issued a report that was probably the first to suggest this notion of a continuum in talking about alcohol problems. Figure 1.1 shows how the Institute of Medicine conceptualized alcohol problems.

The triangle represents the population of the United States. The top leg of the triangle represents the amounts that people in the United States drink. Surprisingly, about one third of Americans don't drink at all; most of these non-drinkers are women. The bottom leg of the triangle represents the degree of negative consequences associated with various amounts of drinking on the top leg of the triangle. The labels on each leg roughly approximate the corresponding terms that are defined below. People move back and forth along the continuum as their drinking and associated consequences change. This is an important idea that will be further considered later in the book.

Drinking Definitions

Hazardous drinking is another term for heavy drinking. Heavy drinking is defined in terms of number of drinks per week and is in contrast to moderate or controlled drinking. While specific drinking amounts have varied from country to country, and research study to research study, in recent years (due largely to excellent work by Martha Sanchez-Craig and her colleagues at the Addiction Research Foundation in Toronto, Canada) a consensus appears to have formed that consumption of more than 14 drinks per week, or more than 4 drinks at a sitting, for men and more than 9 drinks per week, or more than 3 drinks at a sitting, for women constitutes hazardous drinking. It is important to realize that these are "average" or "aggregate" figures that are based on a mythical "average" person. Individuals of different heights and weights, experience with alcohol, with or without medical or other psychological problems will be affected differently by consuming these amounts. Nonetheless, on the average, drinking more than these amounts greatly increases the risk that a person will be harmed.

Harmful drinking is drinking that has actually caused harm, where the harm can clearly be attributed to the alcohol. However, there are some qualifications to this definition. One is that alcohol consumption has been persistent over at least a month or has occurred repeatedly over the course of a year. The other is that the person is not alcohol dependent (see definition, on p.12). This means that a person who is experiencing harmful drinking probably lies somewhere between the person who is alcohol dependent, or alcoholic, and the person who is a moderate drinker.

Moderate (or controlled) drinking is drinking that falls below the quantities and frequencies that define hazardous drinking. Thus, a moderate drinker consumes (if a man) no more than 14 drinks per week, and no more than 4 drinks at a sitting, or (if a woman) no more than 9 drinks per week and no more than 3 drinks at a sitting. Often the term "controlled" drinking is used to refer to a person who has suffered from alcohol dependence or alcoholism who has reduced their drinking to moderate levels.

This definition, as well as the two previous ones, raises the question of what is a "drink"? As with other definitions, this one also varies from country to country. For example, in Japan a "standard" drink contains 28 grams of alcohol, while in the United Kingdom a "standard" drink contains 8 grams.

In the United States, however, there is a more or less generally accepted definition of what is called a "standard" drink that states that a 12-ounce can of beer, a 5-ounce glass of table wine, or 1.5-ounces of 80 proof liquor are all "standard" drinks. That is, they all contain about the same amount of alcohol. When using the term "drink" throughout the rest of this book, I will adopt this definition. So when I speak of a person as being a "moderate" beer drinker, that means a man consumes no more than 14 12-ounce beers per week and a woman consumes no more than 9 12-ounce beers per week.

Our final Drinking Definition is *binge drinking*. As with the previous definitions, this one has numerous forms and is quite controversial. The definition of binge drinking often depends on who is using the definition and in reference to whom. Thus, a widely used definition of binge drinking has grown out of studies of college students and other drinkers who are not alcoholics or alcohol dependent, but whose drinking appears to correspond to the definition of hazardous drinking outlined above. This definition defines a "binge" as consumption of 5 or more drinks on one occasion by a man or 4 or more drinks on one occasion by a woman. Again, the significance of these quantities varies from individual to individual. Thus, consumption of 5 standard drinks by a massive offensive lineman for a professional football team has a different implication for harm than does the consumption of the same 5 drinks by a professional jockey!

Clinically, when speaking about people who have a diagnosable alcohol problem, the term "binge" takes on another meaning. In this context, binge drinking is used to refer to a pattern of drinking in which a person drinks heavily for days or weeks at a time, but then stops drinking, again often for days or weeks at a time. This alternating pattern of drinking and abstinence is often called a binge-drinking pattern. Here, the quantities consumed usually exceed the 5 and 4 drinks referred to in the aforementioned definition of binge, and the person often remains almost continuously intoxicated during the binge-drinking period.

Notably, with the exception of harmful drinking, none of these definitions implies that drinking is or is not harmful to a particular person. The dividing line between harmful and hazardous drinking, between moderate and immoderate drinking, is a fine one—actually one drink more than the levels considered moderate. Consequently, a great deal of confusion exists when applying these definitions to individuals because the definitions fail to take individual differences into account. As we shall see, similar problems plague the Diagnosis Definitions.

Diagnosis Definitions

What is an "alcoholic"? How do I know if a relative or a friend is an "alcoholic"? As with everything else in this field, herein lies the controversy! Most of us use the term "alcoholic" to describe someone whose drinking has created problems for themselves or those around them. Yet, it is clear that drinking problems lie along a continuum of severity and impact on both the person and those around the person. It is important to ask questions like: "Is getting a single DWI citation indicative of 'alcoholism'?" "Is getting drunk at your daughter's wedding indicative of 'alcoholism'?"

As you consider the Diagnosis Definitions below, continue to ask yourself those same sorts of questions. In particular, ask those questions when thinking about your own drinking and that of your loved ones.

Most of us have heard of Alcoholics Anonymous (AA), the largest and most widespread self-help support group for people with alcohol problems. There are a number of others that will be considered in a subsequent chapter. We've also seen portrayals of alcoholics in films, such as "28 Days." People in AA call themselves "alcoholics." But what is the AA definition of "alcoholic"? Isn't it the same as the more formal, medical definitions we will discuss shortly? Interestingly, the answer, despite the beliefs of many to the contrary, is "no." The AA definitions of "alcoholic" and "alcoholism" are not the same as the medical definitions. In fact, the so-called "Big Book" of Alcoholics Anonymous fails to provide a consistent definition of "alcoholic" at all. Rather, the problem drinker, according to the Big Book, takes on this designation by reading the book and identifying with the people whose stories appear therein. For AA, you're an "alcoholic" if you call yourself an "alcoholic." The "stretchiness" of this most familiar definition of problem drinking has contributed to the confusion. So much so that two prominent medical societies—the American Society of Addiction Medicine (ASAM) and the American Psychiatric Association (APA)—have attempted to reduce it by promulgating two quite different Diagnosis Definitions of alcohol problems.

> **"Wine is bottled poetry."**
>
> —ROBERT LOUIS STEVENSON

ASAM Definition of Alcoholism

ASAM put forward its definition of alcoholism in the early 1990s. ASAM defines alcoholism as:

> *a primary, chronic disease with genetic, psychosocial, and environmental factors influencing its development and manifestations. The disease is often progressive and fatal. It is characterized by continuous or periodic impaired control over drinking, preoccupation with the drug alcohol, use of alcohol despite adverse consequences, and distortions in thinking, most often denial.*

This is the prototypical statement of the notion of alcoholism as a "disease," a view that has itself produced much confusion and debate, particularly when it comes to deciding how to help people resolve alcohol problems. Interestingly, despite popular views to the contrary, this is not the view of alcoholism that is contained in the central writings of AA. Bill Wilson, one of the co-founders of AA, was clearly hesitant to call alcoholism a "disease" and uses that term only once or twice in the Big Book. The notion of alcoholism as a "disease" probably stems most directly from the work of researcher E.M. Jellinek in the 1950s, although even Jellinek acknowledged that there were some types of alcohol-related problems that were not diseases, nor did they fit the definition put forward in subsequent years by ASAM.

There are many problems with this widely accepted definition, problems that become manifest when one tries to apply it to a particular case. These problems revolve around the many qualifications in the definition, and the global nature of the terms of the definition that allow it to be applied to almost any alcohol-related problems. For example, the qualification "continuous or periodic" has no specific definition itself. Does periodic mean "once or twice" or more? Likewise, terms such as *denial*, which the ASAM definition's framers go to great lengths to explain in subsequent clarifications that are much longer than the definition itself, have been shown to be problematic by researchers. Thus, while the ASAM definition suggests that denial is characteristic of the "disease of alcoholism," researchers have shown that, in fact, denial is an interpersonal process that seems to occur only when a drinker is confronted by another person telling the drinker that his or her drinking is a problem and should be changed. When the drinker is approached in a less label-focused, confrontational manner, denial is rare (more on this and other research in later chapters).

It is also unclear what is meant by terms such as *impaired control.* While a philosophical discussion of control and how it might be impaired by a disease like alcoholism is beyond the scope of this chapter, it is important to recognize that this concept is not as simple as it seems at first blush. So, for example, it has often been said that "alcoholics" are incompetent to decide on drinking reductions as opposed to abstinence. Yet, it is clear that many, many people who might be called alcoholics make the decision to enter treatment and/or to reduce or stop drinking while in the midst of a heavy drinking episode or its aftermath. At what point does control then become impaired?

Despite these problems, the ASAM definition of alcoholism is consistent with other Diagnosis Definitions in avoiding specific reference to the quantity and frequency of drinking. It also focuses largely on the consequences of drinking rather than the behavior of drinking itself.

The next set of Diagnosis Definitions was put forward by the American Psychiatric Association (APA) in its *Diagnostic and Statistical Manual of Mental Disorders, 4th Edition-Text Revision* (*DSM-IV-TR*) and also de-emphasizes drinking in favor of the consequences associated with drinking. The *DSM-IV* defines two types of alcohol problems under the heading of Psychoactive Substance Use Disorders: Alcohol Abuse and Alcohol Dependence. As these are the standard diagnostic definitions in the United States, we'll discuss them at some length. Before we do, however, a short digression to consider the use of the word "abuse" is in order.

Abusing "Abuse"

We've all heard the terms "substance abuse" or "alcohol abuse" or "drug abuse." These terms have become so broad as to be essentially meaningless in accurately capturing the phenomena we are interested in. These terms have often been used synonymously with "addiction." The confusion surrounding the term "alcohol abuse" has become so great that one of the most prestigious professional journals in the field, the *Journal of Studies on Alcohol*, has found it necessary to disseminate a specific editorial policy for what the term "alcohol abuse" will mean in its journal, and how the term must be used. (Because of the confusions noted previously, the journal has also disseminated a similar policy for the use of the term "binge." They use it only in the sense of prolonged heavy drinking and not to mean 5 or more drinks in a row.) In order to maintain clarity, we will do the same here. When we use the term "alcohol abuse," we will use it only in the Diagnostic Definition sense, which is to indicate that a person meets the criteria to be diagnosed with the *DSM* disorder of Alcohol Abuse. When referring to alcohol use that is problematic but does not result in a diagnosable condition (i.e., Alcohol Abuse or Alcohol Dependence) we will use the terms "misuse" or "hazardous drinking." Let's now turn to a more complete discussion of the Diagnostic Definitions.

How the DSM Works

The *DSM-IV-TR* places all problems related to use of alcohol and other drugs into the larger class of Substance-Related Disorders. Under that heading, the framers of the *DSM-IV-TR* further define two classes of Alcohol-Related Disorders: Alcohol Use Disorders (Alcohol Abuse and Alcohol Dependence) and what they term Alcohol-Induced Disorders. Alcohol Intoxication, Withdrawal, Intoxication Delirium, and Withdrawal Delirium are the most prominent among these. However, nine other disorders that cover the full range of psychological symptoms might also be produced by alcohol. The latter are disorders that are directly related to the toxic effects of excessive alcohol consumption, either on a single occasion or over time.

We are most concerned here with the Alcohol Use Disorders, those that reflect consequences of alcohol use that accumulate over a long period of time but are not necessarily directly caused by the pharmacological toxicity of alcohol.

The *DSM-IV-TR*, like several of its predecessors, uses what some have called a "cookbook" or "Chinese menu" approach to diagnosis. In order to receive a particular diagnosis, a client must meet certain global criteria—the most prominent of which is "clinically significant impairment or distress" resulting from a "maladaptive pattern of substance use." (Global criteria will be discussed in more detail later.) A client must also present one or more of a series of more specific criteria. Not every client who receives a particular diagnosis will necessarily meet the same criteria for the diagnosis as another client. This means that two people who receive a diagnosis of Alcohol Dependence could, conceivably, not meet any of the same criteria for that diagnosis. This allows for (or some would say, creates) great heterogeneity and variability among individuals who receive these diagnoses. The main implication of this variability for the clinician is that knowing that a person carries a diagnosis of Alcohol Dependence reveals little about the details of the person's problems.

Within the Alcohol Use Disorders, there are two categories: Alcohol Abuse and Alcohol Dependence. The general criteria for these disorders are the same as the criteria for other Substance Use Disorders such as Cocaine Abuse, Heroin Dependence or Cannabis (marijuana) Abuse. All substances that create problems are presumed, in a sense, to create the same sorts of problems as each other. Within the *DSM-IV-TR* system, Abuse is presumed to be less severe, and at one time was thought to be a precursor to Dependence. However, a long-term study by psychiatrist George Vaillant of Harvard University found that people who receive a diagnosis of Alcohol Abuse do not typically progress to Alcohol Dependence. Thus, while Alcohol Abuse is less severe (in that the negative consequences elaborated in the diagnosis are less impairing than those for Alcohol Dependence), there is some indication that Alcohol Abuse may be a different sort of disorder than Alcohol Dependence. It seems clear that they both fall along the continuum of alcohol problems defined by the Institute of Medicine, however the dividing line between the two disorders is not always clear.

With these preliminary comments in mind, we're now ready to consider the definitions themselves.

Alcohol Abuse

Alcohol Abuse requires that the person experience one or more of the problems outlined in the boxed material below within a 12-month period. This is usually considered to be the immediately preceding 12 months, but that is not necessary. So, a 45-year-old accountant who had two DWI arrests while in college, but no problems associated with alcohol in the past year, could appropriately be diagnosed with Alcohol Abuse. As we shall see with Alcohol Dependence, the "course" or time factors in the diagnosis have not been incorporated into the Alcohol Abuse diagnosis in as much detail as they are for Alcohol Dependence.

In addition to meeting one or more of the criteria for Alcohol Abuse, the person must also experience "clinically significant impairment or distress" as a result.

Far less is known about the course and prevalence of Alcohol Abuse than is known about Alcohol Dependence. This may be due, in part, to the fact that the people who seek help for alcohol-related problems have experienced far more severe problems than those associated with Alcohol Abuse and usually have a diagnosis of Alcohol Dependence, and it's the people in treatment who are the most accessible to researchers. In treatment settings, you will often find that clinicians use the terms Alcohol Abuse, Alcoholism, and Alcohol Dependence interchangeably, even though this is not correct.

THINGS TO REMEMBER

Criteria for Alcohol Abuse

I. (1 or more criteria for over 1 year)

   A. Role Impairment (e.g., failed work or home obligations)

   B. Hazardous use (e.g., driving while intoxicated)

   C. Legal problems related to alcohol use

   D. Social or interpersonal problems due to alcohol

II. Has never met criteria for Alcohol Dependence

THINGS TO REMEMBER

Criteria for Alcohol Dependence

I. Three or more of the following occurring at any time in the same 12-month period

A. Tolerance to the effects of alcohol as defined by either:

i. need for markedly increased amounts of alcohol to achieve desired effect

ii. markedly diminished effect with continued use of the same amount of alcohol

B. Withdrawal symptoms or use of alcohol to avoid withdrawal.

C. Alcohol is consumed in larger amounts or over longer time periods than was intended.

D. Presence of a persistent desire or unsuccessful attempts to cut down or control alcohol use.

E. A great deal of time is spent drinking, obtaining alcohol or recovering from the effects of drinking.

F. The person gives up important social, work or recreational activities in order to drink or as a result of drinking.

G. Alcohol use continues despite the person knowing that they have a persistent or recurring physical or psychological problem that is likely to be due to or made worse by drinking.

Alcohol Dependence

Alcohol Dependence is by far the most widely used diagnosis applied to people with alcohol problems. When most people think of clinically significant drinking problems, or of the label "alcoholic," they are thinking of problems of the sort that qualify for a diagnosis of Alcohol Dependence.

As with other substance-related disorders, in order to receive a diagnosis of Alcohol Dependence, the individual's drinking must create any of a number of problems.

As with Alcohol Abuse, the presence of these criteria in a client's life must create "clinically significant impairment or distress." The definition of "clinically significant" is never made clear in the *DSM* and this leaves lots of room for clinical judgment in applying the diagnosis. It is also easy to see that these criteria create a very heterogeneous group of people who qualify for a diagnosis of Alcohol Dependence. It is possible, for example, for a person to meet criteria A, B, and C, but not D, E, F, and G and still be diagnosed with Alcohol Dependence. It is also possible for a person to meet criteria E, F, and G, but not A, B, C, and D, and receive a diagnosis of Alcohol Dependence. In addition to the seven basic criteria, of which three must be met in order to receive a diagnosis of Alcohol Dependence,

Alcohol Dependence Specifiers

I. With Physiological Dependence: either tolerance or withdrawal criterion is met.

II. Without Physiological Dependence: neither tolerance nor withdrawal criterion is met.

the *DSM-IV-TR* also includes two "Specifiers." This great variety of symptom and problem patterns among people who qualify for this diagnosis is often forgotten when we refer to people who have this diagnosis.

In practice, it is extremely rare to see someone who qualifies for an Alcohol Dependence diagnosis who does not warrant the qualifier "With Physiological Dependence." This is a result of the fact that virtually all regular users of alcohol develop some degree of tolerance to the effects of alcohol. While there is no hard and fast way of distinguishing this "normal" tolerance from "problem" tolerance, clinicians often use the rule of thumb that in order to diagnose "tolerance" the person must report needing at least 50% more alcohol than before to achieve the same effect or drink 50% more than before without any noticeable increase in effect. So, a person who routinely drank two drinks to achieve the "buzz," they preferred but found after a period of drinking that it now took three drinks to achieve the same "buzz" would meet the criterion for tolerance. If two other criteria of Alcohol Dependence were met, the person would receive a diagnosis of Alcohol Dependence with Physiological Dependence.

In yet another attempt to capture the dramatic variability and heterogeneity present in alcohol problems and problem drinkers, the *DSM-IV-TR* also provides what are called "Course Specifiers" for substance-related disorders.

The Course Specifiers, while intended to clarify the process of recovery from alcohol problems, are actually quite controversial when they are scrutinized. What they essentially imply is that a person can *never* fully recover from Alcohol Dependence. A person who returns to moderate and minimally symptomatic alcohol use still retains the diagnosis, despite the fact that his or her drinking no longer is problematic. Thus, once a person is diagnosed with Alcohol Dependence they have that diagnosis for life. While this is intended to capture the continued risk associated with a resumption of drinking for a person who has met the criteria for Alcohol Dependence, it does not adequately capture the range of possible problem resolutions that have been found by researchers—one of which is a return to moderate, non-harmful and non-dependent drinking. In fact, research suggests that this is a very common outcome among people who resolve drinking problems without treatment (probably the vast majority of people with drinking problems). This leads us to the next important topic for consideration in this chapter: the course of alcohol problems.

Course Specifiers for Alcohol Dependence

I. Early Full Remission: At least one month, but less than a year in which no symptoms of Alcohol Dependence or Abuse are present.

II. Early Partial Remission: At least one month, but less than a year in which one or more symptoms of Alcohol Dependence or Abuse are present, but the person does not meet enough symptoms (3 or more) to qualify for the full diagnosis.

III. Sustained Full Remission: No symptoms of Alcohol Dependence or Abuse have been present for a year or more.

IV. Sustained Partial Remission: Full criteria for Alcohol Dependence or Abuse have not been met for a year or more, but one or more of the criteria for either Abuse or Dependence have been present.

Once a Drunk, Always a Drunk? The Course of Alcohol Problems

For many years it has been conventional wisdom, both among lay people and many professionals in the field, that alcohol problems, once initiated, will almost inevitably result in continued drinking of larger quantities, and the drinker will experience greater and greater problems with alcohol, eventually (again, almost inevitably) suffering severe medical and neurological problems, if not imprisonment and death. In fact, this idea of progressiveness was probably first delineated systematically in the late 18th century by the pioneering American physician Benjamin Rush, the father of American psychiatry and a signer of the Declaration of Independence, who developed what he called the "Moral Thermometer" of alcohol problems. While Rush linked "progression" of problems to the type of alcoholic beverage consumed, the implication is clear—as drinking gets worse, the consequences of drinking get worse, too.

The notion of progression has remained with us into the 21st century. In addition, the belief that alcohol problems are largely inherited has been a prominent idea in the popular and clinical conceptions of alcohol problems. However, research conducted on a variety of groups of problem drinkers (from adolescents and college students to adults) has consistently questioned both of these ideas.

The picture of "progression" that emerges most strongly from the research literature is that "progression" is rare among problem drinkers and that most problem drinkers resolve any problems they experience as a result of drinking. The question that might occur to you at this point is, "Well, what leads to resolution of alcohol problems?" The answer is as complex as the problems and the people who experience them. What does seem to be the case is that problems are most likely to resolve when the person experiences a significant shift in social role expectations (i.e., graduates from high school or college and now must hold down a full-time job, a role that is incompatible with heavy drinking during the week) or life circumstances (i.e., becomes a parent for the first time). Other pathways to problem resolution include responding to expressed concerns by significant others, onset of medical problems with advice from one's physician to cut down or stop drinking, a change in social affiliations, or a geographic move. This list is not exhaustive, and it seems likely that there are as many triggers to resolution of alcohol problems as the people who experience them.

Another popular misconception related to the idea of progression is that once a person becomes alcohol dependent (or "alcoholic") he or she will virtually always and inevitably drink as much as he or she can under any circumstances where alcohol is available. In fact, research done in the early 1970s at Johns Hopkins and Rutgers universities shows clearly that this does not happen. In this research, alcohol dependent drinkers were provided unlimited access to alcohol under conditions in which they were housed in a medically supervised unit, and provided with adequate food and medical care. Although alcohol was made available in unlimited quantities (note that this research could not be done now due to regulations about protecting human subjects that were not in place when these studies were done), the subjects were also often required to engage in various tasks in order to obtain the alcohol. The tasks ranged from simple to fairly demanding, but all could produce, if the subject so chose, as much of the subject's preferred alcoholic beverage as desired.

Conventional wisdom suggests that, under these circumstances, these subjects would drink more and more and more until they passed out, and that the amounts they consumed each day would steadily increase. In fact, this is not what was found at all. Subjects tended to find a "comfort level" of consumption and remain there, not increasing their alcohol intake beyond that level. Likewise, they would often take "vacations" from drinking and not drink at all for several days or weeks. This research suggested that alcohol dependent people would not continuously escalate the amounts they drank and were able to exercise fairly precise control over how much they drank and when.

Just as researchers have questioned the notion of progression, so has the idea that alcohol problems are largely inherited. We all hear about entire families who appear to suffer from alcohol problems, but is this the exception rather than the rule? For years, researchers have searched for a specific genetic basis for alcohol problems, but the findings have been mixed at best. What seems to emerge most clearly from the volumes of research studies is that alcohol problems are heterogeneous in respect to genetic involvement. Some people have a clear genetic predisposition to develop alcohol problems, while others don't appear to have this genetic predisposition. When we look carefully at clinical populations, there are clearly many clients who appear to have no family history of alcohol problems, while others seem to have nothing but alcohol problems in their ancestral background. This "mixed bag" has led Marc Schuckit, a psychiatrist who has studied the genetics of alcohol problems for years, to conclude that genetic factors are, at most, only half the story in the development of alcohol problems. While there appear to be some identifiable risk factors for problems with alcohol, these risk factors are not universal. For example, Schuckit's research has identified a group of children of alcohol-dependent parents who seem to have an innate tolerance to the effect of alcohol. They don't feel as intoxicated when they drink as do others, and this tolerance is present from the time they take their first drink. This allows them to drink more than their peers, but since they don't experience the same intensity of positive feelings from drinking they become prone to drink more in order to "keep up." This increases the likelihood that they will become dependent on alcohol, but not all the children of problem-drinking parents who show this characteristic actually develop drinking problems themselves.

What the research suggests, then, is that genetics and other biological factors increase the risk (or probability) that a particular individual will develop problems as a result of drinking. However, the best we can do with a particular person is to say they have a greater or lesser probability of developing problems based on their genetic and family heritage. We are unable to predict with any degree of certainty whether problems will actually occur. In all likelihood, that's because there is another significant variable in the development of alcohol problems: the environment.

It is clear that environmental influences also play a major role in the development of alcohol problems—at least as significant a role as genetic or biological factors. Such factors as cost and availability of alcohol, for example, play a major role in the nature and type of drinking problems that people develop. Using our own national example of the era of Prohibition in the 1920s and 1930s, the amount of alcohol consumed per capita dropped, as did the prevalence of alcohol-related medical problems such as cirrhosis of the liver. Unfortunately, other problems increased, particularly those associated with the fact that alcohol was illegal to make or use for "non-medicinal" purposes. This led to increased social and legal problems in the form of bootleggers and organized crime that capitalized on the scarcity of a product that was still in high demand.

Treat Me or Lose Me: Is Treatment Necessary to Resolve Alcohol Problems?

Related to the question of the progression or progressiveness of alcohol problems is the question of how most people who experience those problems get over them. It has almost become a mantra in our society that when alcohol and other drug problems reach a certain level of severity (albeit unspecified and, perhaps, unspecifiable), the sufferer will almost always require treatment in order to return to a healthier life that is free of negative consequences associated with drinking. In the 1970s and 1980s an entire industry developed in response to this notion, and the "28 Day Rehab" became the approach of choice in many peoples' minds for helping people overcome problems with drinking. What does research say about this important question?

In the past 20 years, there has been more and more focus on what is termed "spontaneous remission" (or "natural" or "unassisted") recovery from alcohol problems. The notion of natural recovery was not new. In fact, Benjamin Rush, author of the Moral Thermometer, wrote about several such cases as early as 1795. The eventual focus on "natural" recovery was generated largely by the work of epidemiologists who were trying to understand the extent of alcohol problems in the American population. These researchers began to hear stories of people who, at one point in time, had experienced severe problems associated with drinking but later appeared to have stopped drinking without help, or to have reduced their drinking to safe amounts. Depending on the study and the particular population that investigators looked at, it became apparent that the majority of alcohol problems, including Alcohol Abuse and Alcohol Dependence, resolved without the individual seeking formal help of any kind. In fact, it appears that regardless of the drug of interest, people who develop problems with substance abuse are more likely to resolve them on their own than through treatment. This appears to be the case regardless of whether or not the person's substance problems reached a level that warranted a diagnosis.

To Quit or Not? How Do Most People Resolve Alcohol Problems?

Closely related to the notion that treatment is necessary to resolve most alcohol problems is the idea that the only way to effectively put an end to alcohol problems is to initiate and sustain lifelong abstinence from alcohol (and other psychoactive substances as well—with the exception of nicotine and caffeine). The same research that examined "natural" recovery also looked at how these people resolved their alcohol problems. Did most people quit altogether, or did most simply reduce their drinking to the point where they were no longer experiencing problems?

The data are somewhat mixed on this question. However, what is clear is that lifelong abstinence is not the most common resolution of alcohol problems. In fact, the folks who are pointed out as the shining stars of sobriety in meetings of Alcoholics Anonymous and have 10, 20, or 30 years or more of complete abstinence are the dramatic exceptions, rather than the rule. As with virtually everything else about alcohol problems, the actual facts differ quite a bit from popular perceptions and clinical suppositions.

Researchers have found that a final resolution of an alcohol problem takes many forms and depends, in part, on how the individual reached that resolution. There is also a suggestion that there may not be any such thing as a "once and for all, end of story, final" resolution of alcohol problems, at least in terms of achieving lifelong abstinence, for most problem drinkers.

What is clear is that abstinence is a more common resolution among people who undergo treatment, while moderation of drinking to a point at which alcohol is no longer creating negative consequences or symptoms of Alcohol Abuse or Dependence, is the most common route to resolution for those people who resolve drinking problems without treatment.

Part of the confusion about resolution of alcohol problems has come from our focus on alcohol consumption itself as the touchstone characteristic of alcohol problems and their resolution. There has been an assumption (logical at some level, but incomplete) that if you want to get over a drinking problem the best way is simply not to drink—to "Just Say No!" Despite the simple logic of this notion—that a person must drink alcohol in order to suffer from a diagnosable alcohol problem—the symptoms of alcohol problems set down in the *DSM-IV-TR* (with the possible exception of withdrawal) have little direct relationship to the amount or frequency with which the individual drinks. It is largely, though not entirely, true that the more a person drinks, the more likely it is that he or she will experience problems as a result of that drinking. However, there are many, many examples of famous (Winston Churchill comes to mind) and not-so-famous people who drank very large amounts over long periods of time but seemed to suffer no ill effects. Again, the watchword is "heterogeneity." There is no such thing as a "typical" person with alcohol problems. Everyone's problems with alcohol are different from those of other problem drinkers.

Throughout modern history, the debate has raged over the better course of action to resolve alcohol problems: a focus on moderation or a focus on abstinence. In the United States, there have always been treatments and support groups guided by both courses of action. Most recently, Moderation Management (MM) has provided support for people who seek to resolve alcohol problems but who are not sure which is the most viable course for them—abstinence or moderation. The focus of MM is to provide support to any person who develops and implements a plan to resolve a drinking problem that best suits that individual, whether it's focused on abstinence or moderation. The fact of the matter is that we simply have no way to tell in advance who will be successful with which approach, although we do know that people who are strongly committed to one approach, regardless of whether it is abstinence or moderation, appear more likely to achieve their goal. In later chapters we will focus on this issue again, particularly in the context of how best to help people resolve alcohol problems in a lasting way. What is clearly emerging from the past 25 years of research on alcohol problems is that there is no one-size-fits-all answer when it comes to resolving problems associated with drinking.

Different Strokes for Different Folks: Recovery, Relapse, and the Future of Treatment

As our knowledge of the causes, course, and outcomes of alcohol problems has grown through research, the picture that emerges is one of far greater hetero-geneity and variability than of uniformity and consistency. This has led, in recent years, to the notion of matching clients to treatments, encouraging alternative routes to resolution of alcohol problems, and an increasingly popular view (at least among researchers) that the best approach to take in understanding alco-hol problems is "different strokes for different folks." This new approach reached its most recent zenith in the large-scale federally funded research proj-ect called Project M.A.T.C.H.

Project M.A.T.C.H. (M.A.T.C.H. stands for Matching Alcohol Treatment to Client Heterogeneity) grew directly out of research showing that there were lots of different ways that people resolve alcohol problems. The original goal was to define client characteristics (such as age, gender, duration and severity of drink-ing problems, personality variables, motivation, etc.) that would predict a better outcome from one of three treatments that were studied. While the researchers in this were unable to identify specific client characteristics (other than anger and resistance) that were associated with outcome, it seems likely that they were look-ing in the wrong place. Other research has clearly shown different outcomes for different approaches for different people. How Project M.A.T.C.H. failed to find matching characteristics will be a topic for discussion later on when we address specific treatments.

While Project M.A.T.C.H. failed to reach its specific goals, it did prove to be a stepping stone for the development of more broadly applicable approaches, and it opened the door for approaches that are less intensive and intrusive than traditional treatments. In particular, results of Project M.A.T.C.H. showed that a four-session Motivational Enhancement Treatment could produce outcomes comparable to two other 12-session approaches (one based on facilitating client involvement in AA, the other focusing on teaching specific cognitive and behav-ioral skills for recovery).

The future of treatment in this country is now one that is extremely open. Over the past 15 years, research has begun to have a significant impact on what treatment providers do, how they conceive of the best ways to help clients resolve alcohol problems, and the ways in which they approach the task of motivating and assisting change. Of particular importance is a growing recognition that there are many different pathways out of problems with alcohol, and that no sin-gle pathway will be appropriate for everyone. While this will almost certainly make it easier for clients and others who wish to get assistance without formal treatment to find an approach that works for them, it puts an increasing burden on clinicians and counselors to be informed about the various approaches in order to help clients choose their own course. This more individualized approach puts greater pressure on providers to conduct assessments of clients in order to assist in treatment, intervention, and support planning. All of this requires more extensive training and credentialing of clinicians than ever before. It also makes it more difficult for potential clients to select the one that will best suit them.

Unfortunately, as the candy store gets more and more stock, the research that would help clinicians make explicit, helpful recommendations to clients and others who want to change their drinking habits, lags behind. In this book, we take an "experimental" approach to resolving alcohol problems. Based on research findings, we will suggest that the clinician's foremost role, at least in the beginning of a relationship with a client, is to help that client make informed decisions about an initial course of action. We will discuss at length some of the principles of this approach and the research that supports it.

As a preview, the approach we suggest is one that attempts to provide the three factors identified by psychologists Edward Deci and Richard Ryan that are necessary to foster lasting changes in behavior. The three factors are (1) *autonomy support,* an explicit acknowledgement of the client as an autonomous human being who will be the ultimate decision maker in any circumstance regarding drinking and its consequences, (2) a helping *relationship* that is characterized by intense respect for the client, empathy for the client's view of the world (although not necessarily agreement with it), and an emphasis on collaboration and active participation with the client in treatment planning and implementation, and finally (3) *competency enhancement* where necessary. That is, providing the client with opportunities to learn new skills, or rethink old ones, that will enhance movement toward the goals the client has committed to achieving.

Within this framework (abbreviated by the acronym ARC) assisting clients and others to make effective and lasting changes in their behavior in pursuit of a healthier life becomes much easier and less fraught with many of the pitfalls that clients encounter. This approach is based not only in research specific to alcohol problem resolution but on findings from the behavior change and motivational literatures generally. Most importantly, for both practitioners and the clients who make the effort to change problem drinking, we believe the ARC approach will greatly enhance their satisfaction with the outcomes.

Key Terms

Alcohol Abuse. A less serious form of *DSM-IV-TR* alcohol use disorder characterized by interpersonal, social, and vocational problems associated with alcohol abuse.

Alcohol Dependence. The more serious form of *DSM-IV-TR* alcohol use disorder characterized frequently by physical as well as behavioral and psychological symptoms. Often used synonymously with "alcoholic."

Course Specifiers. *DSM-IV-TR* criteria used to describe remission from alcohol use disorders.

Recommended Reading

Diagnostic and Statistical Manual of Mental Disorders, 4th Edition (text revision), by the American Psychiatric Association (Washington, DC: Author, 2000).

"Alcohol Use Disorders," by B. S. McCrady (2001), in *Clinical Handbook of Psychological Disorders, 3rd Edition,* edited by D. H. Barlow (pp. 376–433, New York: Guilford).

TRUTH OR FICTION

QUIZ ANSWERS

1. False   2. False   3. False   4. False

CHAPTER 2

Identifying Alcohol Problems: "I Know It When I See It! Or Do I?"

After reading this chapter, you will be able to answer true or false to the following statements:

TRUTH OR FICTION QUIZ

1. Heavy drinking is relative to the drinker and to social and cultural norms. True or False?
2. Problem drinking almost always results in obvious negative consequences for the drinker. True or False?
3. Because problem drinkers are usually in denial, the best source of information about whether drinking is a problem is a spouse or significant other. True or False?
4. When a person denies having a drinking problem, they probably do. True or False?
5. People with alcohol problems are often self-medicating some other psychological problem. True or False?

Answers on p. 38.

In Chapter 1, we reviewed the very confusing world of definitions, symptoms, course, and resolutions of alcohol problems. If you're not completely discouraged by the extreme variability and uncertainty regarding these significant issues in human life, then read on. The murkiness will be cleared (at least a bit) in this chapter.

The main issue for clinicians and others who show concern for a person whose drinking may be causing problems is, "How do I know that this person has an alcohol problem?" There are many answers to this question, and the sources of information that a clinician may rely on are varied, and not always objectively accurate. It's important, therefore, for clinicians to have a clear idea of what to look for, how to approach clients about their drinking, and how to help significant others understand the client's drinking. The problem here, though, is that *there are no universally reliable indicators of alcohol-related problems.*

As with virtually everything else in this field, there is much mythology and folklore about how to identify, understand, and intervene with alcohol problems.

We saw some of this in Chapter 1, and in this chapter we will consider some popular conceptions that have been challenged by research. The goal of this chapter will be to take some of the confusing information presented in Chapter 1 and fashion it into a conceptual framework within which you can begin to think about the drinking of others, and to develop an understanding of how to productively raise this with the drinker in a way that will facilitate healthy decision making and possibly change.

Signs and Symptoms: Fleshing Out the *DSM*

The Big Book of AA states that whether or not a person is an "alcoholic" is a matter of personal self-evaluation and decision. By reading the stories in the Big Book and identifying with one or more of the accounts, a person can decide whether or not to accept the "alcoholic" label and begin the process of change by following the 12 steps.

In clinical practice, however, we are faced with a different task than the person who is concerned with a possible drinking problem and reads the Big Book. The clinician's task is to identify problems or potential problems in others and then share our perceptions in a way that will facilitate client decision-making in addressing those problems. But it is this "external" view by the clinician that a client has a problem with alcohol that is, at once, the most important observation a clinician can make and the source of many of the problems encountered in working with clients whose drinking is problematic. We will address this more in later chapters. In this chapter, we will focus on how to identify alcohol problems in our clients and how to do so in a way that will lead to a constructive, therapeutic approach to those problems that the client will accept and not resist. Here we will focus on "informal" signs, rather than on the diagnostic criteria or specific standard screening and assessment procedures.

> **"I shall not today attempt further to define the kinds of material I understand to be embraced...[b]ut I know it when I see it..."**
>
> —U.S. SUPREME COURT JUSTICE POTTER STEWART, ASKED TO DEFINE "PORNOGRAPHY"

There have been many guides for clinicians and "concerned significant others" (CSOs) such as family members and employers on how to read the signs that suggest a person's drinking may be problematic. In fact, many clients are initially pressured to seek consultation by a CSO who views the client's drinking as being problematic. For the clinician, however, it can be very difficult identifying client drinking problems without formal assessment. There are several reasons why this is so: (1) There are no universally accurate behavioral indicators of alcohol problems or even alcohol intoxication. Nor are there any universally reliable laboratory tests that can diagnose problem drinking; (2) Clinicians rarely see their clients in situations in which alcohol is consumed; therefore they don't have first-hand knowledge of how much a client drinks or the effect alcohol has on a client;

(3) Likewise, they rarely see their clients intoxicated; (4) Even if the client is open about how much and how often they drink and the clinician is knowledgeable about such data as "safe" and "harmful" drinking patterns, applying that knowledge to a particular client is more complex than simply saying "you're drinking (some number of) drinks every day, and that suggests a problem."

Often CSOs believe that drinking is excessive when, in the context of both the diagnostic criteria for alcohol use disorders, and in the degree of negative consequences associated with drinking, no diagnosis is warranted. CSOs typically focus on quantity and frequency of drinking, using their own personal standards for how much is "too much." They often will recall one or two highly salient instances of misbehavior by the client in which alcohol was involved in some way and attribute the misbehavior (sometimes correctly, sometimes not) to the drinking. It is the clinician's job to try to make sense of these perceptions, honestly made and reported but often erroneous. That is not to say that CSOs aren't a highly useful source of information about potential client drinking problems, or that CSOs are unreliable observers. Rather, it is our intention to point out that a drinking problem, like Potter Stewart's pornography, is sometimes in the eye of the beholder.

Let's look at this problem in more detail. As mentioned in Chapter 1, quantity and frequency are one aspect of alcohol problems, but not the whole story. It is important to recognize that the data clinicians have available from research about "safe" and "harmful" levels of drinking, are *average* data based on large samples of diverse individuals. Within these samples, and in the general population of drinkers, there is a fair amount of diversity in terms of how various quantity/frequency combinations affect other aspects of the client's life. So, what may appear to be "heavy" or even "alcoholic" drinking for one person may not, in fact, be a harmful pattern. Conversely, clients may overestimate the degree of problems associated with their drinking and believe that their drinking is problematic when, in fact, it isn't. Two examples serve to illustrate this difficulty.

The Case of Mary

Mary was a 68-year-old retired teacher who had never married, but had lived a very full life revolving around her profession and several very close friends, with whom she often traveled. A few months prior to coming to see one of us, Mary's best friend and travel companion died suddenly of a heart attack. Mary began, she thought, to develop a drinking problem and, not wanting to become an "alcoholic," sought a consultation to help her decide what to do about it. Our initial assessment revealed that Mary, as was often the case with persons in her generation, drank two cocktails daily before dinner. She had done so for more than 40 years. She was not a wine drinker and rarely consumed more than her two nightly cocktails. She was in excellent health and had never had any alcohol-related negative consequences in her life.

Following her friend's death, Mary began to drink an additional cocktail before dinner, often finishing her drink while she ate. What concerned Mary was not the additional drink, but that she decided that her drinking was having consequences she did not like (e.g., falling asleep in front of the TV and waking up with a slight hangover). She found it difficult to roll back her drinking to two drinks per day. This difficulty, combined with the fact that her drinking had increased, convinced Mary that she probably was developing a drinking problem and prompted her to seek help. However, a thorough screening and assessment (specific screening and assessment instruments and methods are described in Chapter 3) revealed only a single *DSM* symptom of alcohol dependence (difficulty quitting or cutting down). Mary was neither an alcohol abuser, nor alcohol dependent. She was, however, a victim of some of the myths about drinking problems that are common in our society.

The Case of Tom

Tom was a 35-year-old divorced man who was referred for an alcohol evaluation by a Family Service social worker. Tom's ex-wife had be granted custody of their two boys, ages 9 and 11, but she had subsequently developed a severe drug problem that required her to be hospitalized for treatment. Tom had applied through the State Family Service agency (which had placed the boys in temporary foster care) to regain custody of his boys. The social worker who referred Tom did a thorough custody interview, which included a query about alcohol use. Tom readily acknowledged that he drank and described the following pattern: After work he would come home and have two or three cans of beer while he prepared dinner. He'd drink another can or two with dinner, and after dinner, he would typically finish off the six pack while watching TV. To the social worker, who was a petite, non-drinking woman, this sounded like an extraordinary amount of alcohol to consume, and it seemed even more significant when Tom acknowledged that this pattern occurred daily. Not wanting to be unfair, however, she referred Tom for a full evaluation.

When Tom walked through my office door, I immediately could see that he was not a "typical" person. He was 6 feet 8 inches tall and must have weighed close to 300 pounds. Tom told me that he had played offensive line in college and had even spent a couple of years with a local professional football team. He was a BIG guy! After getting an account of his drinking, I brought out my blood alcohol tables, and we estimated what Tom's blood alcohol content (BAC) would be after a typical day's drinking. We had to estimate, because the tables only covered men up to a weight of 280 pounds. His typical drinking day (six 12-ounce beers over the course of 3 to 4 hours) resulted in a peak of .04%, or less than half the legal limit for driving in most states, and even below the level that most social drinkers typically reach. Further assessment revealed that Tom had never experienced any negative consequences associated with his drinking. He met neither criteria for alcohol abuse nor alcohol dependence.

These cases demonstrate the dangers of jumping to conclusions about the presence of an alcohol problem on the basis of an incomplete assessment or none at all. That being said, a clinician seeing a client for the first time should be alert to a number of red flags that are often associated with problems with alcohol. These red flags should prompt a more thorough assessment using the techniques reviewed in Chapter 4. These red flags become even more useful if clinicians make it a habit to question *all* new clients about drinking and drinking-related consequences.

Problem drinking can also take a wide variety of forms. It is clear that the stereotypic image of the problem drinker or alcohol-dependent person as being chronically drunk and living a disorganized, disrupted life is a false stereotype. Many problem drinkers drink only intermittently. Two broad drinking patterns seem to be associated with alcohol problems: regular or chronic drinking, and so-called "binge" drinking.

Regular drinkers tend to drink daily or nearly so. They often have difficulty cutting down or stopping and may experience both high tolerance and withdrawal symptoms when they attempt to stop drinking. These are often the easiest problems for drinkers to detect, as they are most likely to have pervasive, lasting negative consequences as a result of drinking.

Binge drinkers, on the other hand, may go for weeks or months without drinking at all, only to initiate a daily routine of heavy drinking that can last weeks or months. For binge drinkers, stopping drinking is not an issue (or at least they may not see it as an issue!). They do it all the time. For binge drinkers, this main issue is identifying and forestalling the onset of a binge and ending it as quickly as possible. Distinguishing chronic patterns from binge drinking is critical in treatment planning, especially when the client is being treated for a co-occurring psychological disorder.

So what does the "typical" problem drinker look like? The typical client with alcohol problems, if there is a typical client, is a middle-class, largely functional family man or homemaker who comes to treatment for something other than a drinking problem (Schuckit, 2004).

1. Client is male. Men develop alcohol problems at about three times the rate of women, with data suggesting that between 5% and 25% of male drinkers will have some alcohol-related problems during their lifetime. The rate of alcohol problems in men who have co-occurring psychiatric disorders, such as depression, is even higher. This does not mean that women should not be screened for alcohol problems but that men are much more likely to have such problems.

2. Client is a young adult. The rates of alcohol problems are highest in young adult males between the ages of 18 and 30. That does not mean that clients with other age and gender characteristics do not develop alcohol-related problems but that being a young adult places one in a very high risk group for development of alcohol-related problem.

3. Client has one or more of the following complaints: insomnia, sadness and depression, anxiety, or interpersonal problems. While not all clients with these problems will also have problems with alcohol, the prevalence of alcohol problems in clients who present with these symptoms is several times that of the general population.

4. History reveals that the client often misses work or neglects other activities, particularly on Monday mornings (often because of recovering from weekend drinking).

5. Client reports using drugs other than alcohol, including cigarettes. Epidemiologic research has shown that people who use drugs other than alcohol are between 20 to 25 times more likely than non-drug users to also have alcohol-related diagnoses (Grant & Dawson, 1999).

When one or more of these symptom patterns is revealed by an intake interview, the clinician should be sure to inquire further and consider a more thorough assessment.

Family members can be a useful source of information, as well, and when family members report to the therapist that their loved one is "drinking too much" this can also serve as a red flag to prompt more thorough assessment. As we have seen, however, it is important that the therapist not reach a conclusion based solely on a family member's assertion of a "drinking problem." It is easy to point to drinking as the cause of other problems (interpersonal, sexual, vocational) that may be more subtle in their manifestations. Even when a family member or other important person in the client's life suggests that the client is a problem drinker, the clinician needs to be prepared to do his or her own assessment.

> "One man's meat is another man's poison."
>
> —PROVERB

Recognizing More than One Problem: Is It Just a Drinking Problem?

As we noted in the last section, it is commonplace for clients whose drinking is problematic to come to treatment for some other psychological complaint. In addition, clients with medical problems associated with drinking often will bring them to their primary care physician. For this reason, obtaining recent medical records when the therapist suspects the possibility of an alcohol-related problem can be very useful. It is also helpful for the therapist to become familiar with the wide variety of medical consequences that may be associated with alcohol misuse. Clients who report having, for example, liver problems, pancreatitis or other gastrointestinal complaints should be routinely asked about their drinking (for a compendium of medical consequences of both alcohol and drug use, see Brick, 2003).

The basic rule of thumb is to screen for alcohol problems in all clients, not just ones who come specifically complaining of alcohol problems. To acknowledge alcohol-related problems is still quite stigmatizing in our society, and it behooves the therapist to recognize that clients will not always be immediately forthcoming about their drinking, unless specifically asked about it.

How Likely is the Problem Drinker to Have Other Problems?

The question of co-morbidity of alcohol problems with other disorders has been extensively studied. While the precise degree of co-morbidity varies from study to study (due largely to both differing methodologies and different study samples) it is clear that persons who suffer alcohol-related problems have a much higher likelihood of having other psychiatric or medical problems than those who do not. Depending on the specific psychiatric disorders (e.g., depression, bipolar disorder, anxiety disorders) the likelihood that a person with an alcohol problem will have another *DSM-IV-TR* diagnosis ranges from 15% to more than 50% (Grant & Dawson, 1999).

Stated in terms of odds ratios (the likelihood that a person with a *particular DSM-IV-TR* diagnosis will also have either a current or lifetime [at any time in his or her life] alcohol-related diagnosis), clients with major depression are 2 to 3 times more likely than clients without this problem. Clients who suffer from bipolar disorder with manic features are nearly five times as likely to have alcohol-related problems as those with no psychiatric disorder. The most highly co-morbid *DSM-IV-TR* diagnosis with alcohol problems is Antisocial Personality Disorder with these clients being more than 10 times more likely to have problems with alcohol than persons without this disorder.

One large-scale study, the Epidemiologic Catchment Area study (Robins, Locke, & Regier, 1990), suggests that, on average, one-third or more of clients coming to psychiatric services for help with psychiatric problems also have alcohol-related problems. This suggests that it is virtually impossible for clinicians to avoid having to confront these problems on some level.

"Denial" May Be Just a River in Egypt: Where Does Denial Come From?

One of the concerns often voiced by clinicians when the subject of identifying clients with alcohol problems arises is, "Won't they minimize or conceal their problems as a result of 'denial'?" Certainly, clients with alcohol- and other substance-related problems will often appear to minimize or deny the nature and extent of their problems, particularly when confronted by a therapist or significant other about their drinking problem. In fact, as we saw in Chapter 1, some definitions of "alcoholism" place such an emphasis on this behavior of denial that it is included as a central and defining feature of the disorder (or disease, if you prefer). Denial is considered by these definitions (as well as many writers in the field who subscribe to traditional views of alcohol problems; e.g., Milam & Ketcham, 1984) to be a characteristic of the disease of alcoholism and may extend to people whose drinking has not yet reached dependent levels but who are experiencing alcohol-related difficulties. Ironically, this has led to a veritable Catch-22 for clients whose drinking is creating problems. On the one hand, if they acknowledge that their drinking is causing problems, they risk being told that the only way to address them is total lifelong abstinence (regardless of the severity of the problems), something for which they may not be prepared. On the other hand, clients who do not acknowledge that their drinking is a problem are labeled as being "in denial," and this very fact is used as evidence that their drinking is much more problematic than the client is willing to acknowledge.

So, if it is true that people with alcohol problems are in denial, how can a clinician expect to get accurate data from such clients. And without accurate data, how can the clinician responsibly and reasonably address the clinical issues presented by such clients?

The answer comes from research on human dyadic communication that was extensively reviewed in the mid–1980s by William Miller (Miller, 1985), one of the originators of an approach to clients with problem drinking that is called "motivational interviewing" (discussed more deeply in a later chapter).

> "He is a drunkard who takes more than three glasses though he be not drunk."
>
> —EPICTETUS (50–120 A.D.)

Miller, who was trained in both behavioral and Rogerian psychotherapy approaches, was working with clients with alcohol and drug problems as a young psychologist. In staff meetings, he would listen to the accounts of other therapists and counselors in which clients were repeatedly characterized as being in denial about the nature and extent of the drinking problems the therapist, or others, believed they had. What puzzled Miller was that he, in contrast to his colleagues (who were often much more experienced in working with alcoholic clients), rarely encountered denial from his clients. His clients seemed to be pretty much the same as those his colleagues were seeing, so why was Miller not getting the same patterns of denial and resistance to acknowledging problems associated with drinking that his colleagues reported?

The answer, Miller proposed in his 1985 review, was that denial was not a characteristic of the client or of a disease process. Rather, it was a predictable result of a particular type of communication pattern between client and therapist.

Miller cited decades of research in social psychology on dyadic communication in which researchers had developed the construct of *psychological reactance*. Psychological reactance occurred whenever a particular type of communication dyad was set up in the laboratory with normal subjects. The communication pattern that created reactance was one in which one person, A, gave a second person, B, a directive communication to change a behavior about which B was ambivalent. That is, the behavior that A directed B to change was one that B both valued and wished to continue. But B also recognized the negative consequences attached to it and that the behavior might very well need to be changed. When this communication dyad was established, B's response to A's directive to change was almost universally to resist the change, that the behavior was not a problem, and, sometimes, that A should mind her own business!

From Miller's observations, this communication pattern was prototypical of the style of communication that alcohol counselors and other clinicians used with their clients. Part of the standard approach by counselors at that time (and in many programs this is still true) was to attempt to persuade the client to accept the label "alcoholic," often by forcefully confronting the client with all of the problems drinking had presumably caused.

The reasoning behind this attempt came from an interpretation of the 12-step literature of Alcoholics Anonymous (AA) and the AA practice of inviting members to stand up at meetings and identify themselves as alcoholics ("Hi, I'm Bill, and I'm an alcoholic."). It was believed that if clients engaged in this confession, they would be well on the way to overcoming their drinking problems. As a result, this process became enshrined as a cornerstone of traditional substance abuse treatments.

For Miller, this represented exactly the pattern that elicited psychological reactance. Not being a traditionally trained alcoholism counselor, Miller avoided the strategy of attempting to persuade clients to adopt an often pejorative label. He simply asked them about their drinking, what bothered them about it, what bad things happened when they were drinking, and what, if anything, they thought they might want to do about it. And, lo and behold, no denial!

Armed with the insight that a therapist could reduce or eliminate denial simply by communicating in ways that did not foster it, Miller began to systematize a very different approach to clients with alcohol problems that he called "motivational interviewing" (Miller & Rollnick, 1993; 2003). This approach has proven so successful in overcoming the sorts of denial and resistance that counselors were seeing (fostering) in their clients that it has become mainstream.

So, if therapist behavior creates denial, and the specific behaviors responsible can be identified, then the therapist can change those behaviors in ways that minimize denial and maximize the chances of eliciting an accurate and useful account of drinking and associated problems from the client. This is a very optimistic message.

What Should I Do as a Professional? Roles and Responsibilities

You've discovered that a client may be drinking in a harmful or dependent fashion. What should you do? This section offers some suggestions. These suggestions are not hard and fast rules but rather guidelines to assist you in structuring how you approach your client about his or her drinking.

1. *Be respectful.* As a therapist you may share some of the negative stereotypes of persons with alcohol problems that are common in our society. It's important that you identify these stereotyped ideas, recognize that you have them, and make every effort to overcome them. Respect for your client is critical, as is an operating assumption that your client is capable of making effective decisions about his or her drinking, if given the opportunity. Assume your client is capable of making healthy decisions, until it is clearly demonstrated otherwise.

2. *Be empathetic and non-prescriptive.* Clients with alcohol problems often avoid getting help because of the stigma attached to having problems with alcohol and the fear that they will be forcefully told that all drinking (as well as other substance use) must stop immediately. Remember, a client who is drinking a lot is doing so for some payoff. Giving up alcohol without a viable alternative to achieving some of the goals served by drinking can be frightening to a client. Empathize and respect the client's ambivalence about change.

3. *If the client appears to be an imminent danger to self or others, the usual professional reporting and action obligations apply.* However, you should implement these along *with* the client, not to the client, if at all possible. To the extent that you can work in a persuasive rather than prescriptive manner, you will enhance the likelihood that your client will respond appropriately. You will also provide your client with a positive treatment experience, something that will increase the likelihood that the client will continue to work with you.

4. *Be alert to a need for medically supervised detoxification.* Keeping your client safe is critical. The rule of thumb for suggesting medically supervised and assisted detox is daily consumption of six or more standard drinks over a span of more than three months. Alcohol is the one of the few substances that people become dependent upon (other than benzodiazepines, such as Valium or Xanax) that carries with it a risk of grand mal seizures and possible death if heavy, chronic use is stopped suddenly. For those clients who are drinking six or more drinks per day, it should be automatic that you refer them to a physician to assist in detox. The detox does not have to be done in an inpatient setting. Most detoxes can be accomplished on an ambulatory basis, so the establishment of relationships with local physicians who can manage ambulatory detox is an important part of professional practice with clients who have drinking problems.

5. *Be very aware of confidentiality and information transmission regulations, both state and federal.* Substance abuse treatment information has

greater protection under federal confidentiality laws (42 CFR Part 2) than does other medical information.

6. *If you are not going to address your client's drinking directly in your treatment, be aware of local providers who can do so and make a referral to one or more of them.* Your role in this case should be to provide a range of options that your client can explore, not coerce the client into a treatment that he or she finds unacceptable.

7. *Lastly, continue to work with your client, even while he or she is in treatment for drinking with another clinician.* Maintaining a strong, working alliance with your client and being supportive through detox and beyond will help ensure that your client sticks with the change process.

How Drinking Affects Family, Work, and Other Areas of the Client's Life

It is important when exploring drinking-related negative consequences with your client to understand that not all consequences may be due solely to drinking. Drinking problems occur in a context. Given the stigma and negative views of drinkers that are still held by many in our society, it is important to consider the context as well as actual client behaviors in attempting to understand the impact of drinking on a person's life.

Family and Social Problems

The most commonly affected areas in a client's life, at least early on in the development of problem drinking, tend to be family and social relationships. Clients will report expressions of disapproval of their drinking from family members, spouses, romantic partners, and friends (although depending on the client's social milieu, friends may, in fact, encourage heavy drinking). In fact, research suggests that the main reason for seeking help for a drinking problem is pressure or concern from family, spouse, or a concerned significant other (CSO). Changes in behavior of the client toward CSOs, particularly when the client is drinking or intoxicated, are often the main source of conflict early in the development of problem drinking. Of course, violence or aggressive behavior associated with alcohol is critical to assess and intervene with your client, but alcohol use may also impact on conjugal relationships by dampening sexual response (particularly in males) or making intimate interactions unappealing to the client's partner. Exploring these consequences with the client and, when possible, also speaking to the CSO can help flesh out the picture of how alcohol is affecting the client's social relationships.

One caveat is in order, however. As noted above, the context of drinking and related problems is important in understanding negative consequences. CSOs are part of the context, and their own attitudes about drinking and alcohol consumption will play a role in the degree of conflict about those behaviors with the client. A CSO who is a non-drinker is more likely to see even small amounts of alcohol consumption as problematic than is a CSO who is a regular (but not problematic) drinker.

Social problems may also extend to legal difficulties. These can range from relatively minor, but quite costly problems, such as a DWI arrest and conviction, to assaultive behavior and even homicide. In fact, when researchers have studied the relationship between drug intoxication and criminal behavior, it is alcohol, not illicit drugs, that is most strongly associated with aggressive and violent behavior in users of the drug. Unfortunately, it is often legal problems that prompt problem drinkers to seek treatment. In such cases, establishing a clear set of role boundaries with the client regarding what will and will not be shared with legal authorities about treatment is critical to gaining the client's trust and cooperation with behavior change efforts.

Work Problems

Clients who are drinking a lot often also experience problems at work. Chronic lateness, excessive use of sick time (particularly on Mondays), and changes in mood and behavior on the job are often associated with problematic drinking. With the client's permission, speaking to his/her employer can be helpful in understanding not only the pattern of consequences, but also in fleshing out a picture of the client's drinking. It can also be helpful in treating the client to elicit cooperation from the employer. One well-researched and validated treatment approach—community reinforcement training—often includes employers as part of treatment (Smith & Meyers, 1999).

Health and Medical Consequences

The most significant consequences of alcohol problems over the long term are often medical. Without going into a detailed discussion here, there are a number of medical conditions that are either caused by or exacerbated by heavy alcohol consumption. These include a variety of upper gastrointestinal tract problems (such as esophagitis or esophageal varices), liver problems, pancreatic problems (the single most common cause of pancreatitis is heavy alcohol consumption), hypertension (alcohol consumption raises blood pressure), and diabetes. Longer term, very heavy alcohol consumption is also a causal factor in a number of alcohol-related neurological problems, particularly Wernicke-Korsakoff syndrome and other alcohol-related dementias. Alcohol interferes with absorption of B vitamins, and thus various neurological problems stemming from B vitamin deficiency are also possible in long-term heavy drinkers.

Acute or sudden cessation of drinking after a prolonged period of heavy consumption can result in both grand mal seizures and delirium tremens. The latter has its onset some time after cessation of drinking, if it is going to occur, typically about 72 hours following the last drink. Thus, even if a client has stopped drinking recently, it is still important to be alert for the emergence of alcohol-related withdrawal problems.

"So, What's In It For Me?" Answering Questions from Clients about Treatment

This is perhaps the most difficult section of this chapter to write in a charitable, straightforwardly informative way. This is because much of what happens in many treatment settings is directly counter to what research suggests is most effective in helping problem drinkers make the decision to change, and then pursuing change goals they, themselves, have committed to.

More than three decades of research has shown that there is no single approach to working with alcohol problems that is effective with every client. Nonetheless, when clients with alcohol problems are identified and referred to treatment, they almost always receive a treatment that is based on a single set of theoretical principles. They are rarely, for example, offered medication as a treatment aid, despite the fact that there are at least two medications (disulfiram and naltrexone) that research has shown to be effective in helping some clients with alcohol problems. Likewise, virtually all programs insist that the client adopt the goal of lifelong abstinence with respect to alcohol and all other drugs as a condition of entering and remaining in treatment. Aside from the failure of this "one size fits all" approach to address the extreme diversity among clients with alcohol-related problems, this philosophy has severely limited our ability to effectively treat a broad range of clients and attract them into treatment.

That being said, engaging clients whose drinking has caused them problems in a change process has clear advantages. In answering the question posed at the beginning of this section, it may be better for the clinician to speak to the issue of "what's in it for me if I change my drinking?" rather than endorsing any particular route toward making those changes. Self-help groups, books, treatment, or unaided efforts to change have all been shown to produce results with some clients. When this broader and more client-centered approach is taken, the conversation becomes much easier to manage.

So, what is in it for the client if he or she changes? The answer depends on what sorts of negative consequences are associated with drinking and how important it is to the client to avoid those consequences in the future. For a client whose drinking produces occasional hangovers curable by popping a few aspirin, the importance of continuing to use alcohol may be greater than changing, especially if change is portrayed as meaning abstinence. For another client whose drinking is creating significant social, vocational, or legal difficulties, change—including abstinence—may seem highly worthwhile but may also seem too difficult to achieve.

Answering the question must therefore focus on three factors: (1) The client's perception of the seriousness and importance of the negative consequences associated with alcohol consumption; (2) The client's perception of the benefits of continuing unchanged versus making some changes aimed at eliminating negative consequences; and (3) The client's confidence in his or her ability to make the necessary changes and how his/her life will improve should those changes be made. One way to begin the discussion of these factors is through completing a Decisional Balance Worksheet (see Figure 2.1) with the client. The clinician and client collaboratively lay out the pros and cons of change versus remaining the same. Simply doing this easy exercise can be highly motivating to clients.

The Decisional Balance Worksheet exercise is completed with the client offering as many entries into each quadrant of the matrix as possible. The clinician guides the process by asking questions and selecting the starting point. In Figure 2.1, the small numbers in the lower right hand corner of each quadrant indicate the order in which the quadrants should be addressed. The clinician starts off by addressing the Advantages ("Pros") of Not Changing, for example, continuing unchanged, or the "good things" about continuing to drink as before. Discussion then moves to the Disadvantages ("cons") of Change as the client sees them, then to the Disadvantages of Not Changing, and finally to the Advantages of Changing. This sequence is based on research that has shown that clients who ultimately make changes do so because the Advantages of Change appear greater to them than the advantages of remaining unchanged. Clients who decide to change still recognize advantages to remaining the same, but see something better ahead if a change is made.

Once the clinician has helped the client sort out the advantages and disadvantages of change, generally, then the discussion can proceed to the issue of how to change. As we have indicated, there are many different pathways to changing and reducing alcohol-related problems. Again, using a Decisional Balance Worksheet, the clinician can collaboratively assist the client in determining which of many options makes the most sense right now for the client, given his or her life circumstances. If the balance tips in favor of treatment, the clinician might then begin a discussion of what treatment programs are available in the geographic area where the client lives.

	Pros	Cons
Change	4	2
Don't Change	1	3

Figure 2.1: Sample Decisional Balance Worksheet for changing vs. not changing.

Numbers refer to the order in which cells are to be filled.

So, the bottom line for answering "what's in it for me" is that the answer is likely to be unique to each client. It is the clinician's role to help clients lay out the arguments for and against change in a systematic, non-prescriptive, non-judgmental fashion. By doing so the clinician facilitates the client's own decision making and enhances the likelihood that the client will be comfortable making a strong commitment to the change options selected.

To Refer or Not to Refer: Advantages and Disadvantages of Referring a Client to Specialized Treatment

Given the limitations of the current specialized treatment system noted in the previous section, the clinician faced with a client whose drinking has created significant negative consequences may feel in a quandary. One the one hand, it is unlikely that most treatment programs will provide truly individualized treatment for clients, and it is virtually certain that specialized treatment programs will not accept a client goal of reducing drinking rather than total abstinence. On the other hand, research suggests that, for clients who are willing to commit themselves to the tasks associated with specialized treatment, successful change is highly likely to occur, at least over the short term.

This quandary suggests that clinicians need to be both thoroughly conversant with the specialized treatment programs in their area and to also be aware of and willing to suggest alternatives in cases where clients are resistant, at least at the time of discussion of formalized treatment, to entering a treatment program.

In most cases, the decision to refer should be made, as should all other decisions about client care, in close collaboration with the client. Options should be discussed objectively with both pros and cons of particular options being reviewed to the client's satisfaction. While the clinician should behave with the client's welfare uppermost in mind, it is important that the clinician recognize that the client's idea of his or her welfare and best interests may differ from the clinician's. The tack that we recommend clinicians take is to make recommendations (we prefer the term "suggestions") to clients conservatively at the beginning. It is our policy to always suggest initially in discussing options with clients that abstinence as a drinking goal may be the healthiest route, at least in the short run. That being said, the process of deciding what to do should be accomplished with the client, rather than prescriptively and paternalistically. In our experience, when clients are engaged in this collaborative fashion, they more often than not choose courses of action that are beneficial and healthier for themselves. It is when clients feel coerced into a course of action that resistance occurs and reactance is likely. Even with clients who are referred by an outside coercive authority (courts, probation/parole officers, employers, etc.) this collaborative approach with systematic weighing of pros and cons bears fruit more readily than a prescriptive, paternalistic approach.

Summing Up

The process of identifying clients with alcohol problems and helping them make a decision to change their drinking is clearly both subtle and complex. There are no easy answers for the clinician. The basic principles that apply, though, are clear. When clinicians work with clients in an autonomy-supportive fashion, within the context of a respectful and empathetic therapeutic relationship, and support the client's own decision-making process, the likelihood of the client successfully beginning a process of healthy change is greatly increased.

The role of the therapist in this process is one of resource and supportive coach. The goal is to help the client decide on a healthy course of action (although that course may not always move the client to full and complete health!) and make a strong commitment to implementing changes. It is critical that the clinician keep in mind that there are many ways in which people overcome drinking problems, and that one size does not fit all (see Anne Fletcher's wonderful book *Sober for Good* for a compendium of first person accounts of the variety of paths to resolving alcohol-related problems).

Key Terms

Problem recognition. The degree to which a person who is drinking is creating negative consequences acknowledges a "problem" with drinking, or recognizes the connection between negative consequences of drinking, but does not label his/her drinking a "problem." Accepting the label "problem" is not necessary for effective change.

Decisional balance. Exercise in which the client and therapist explore the good things ("pros") and not so good things ("cons") of drinking and changing drinking. Most effective when done in a nondirective fashion simply asking the client to fill in the Decisional Balance Worksheet.

Consequences of drinking. Negative events in any life sphere (family, work, health, interpersonal relationships, legal, etc.) that are directly associated with the individual's drinking. These events are not necessarily indicative of a diagnosable problem but are often the impetus for seeking help.

TRUTH OR FICTION

QUIZ ANSWERS

1. True   2. False   3. False   4. False

CHAPTER 3

Finding and Getting the Best Out of Professional Resources

TRUTH OR FICTION

After reading this chapter, you will be able to answer true or false to the following statements:

1. There is no way to find professional resources without being one yourself. True or False?

2. Any professional should be able to "click with" and treat any client. True or False?

3. It is possible to help clients overcome their resistance to accepting treatment even the first time you meet with them. True or False?

4. Family members and friends are always more of a hindrance than a help. True or False?

5. It is never possible to predict or prevent a crisis situation, you just have to deal with it. True or False?

Answers on p. 58.

Developing a Professional Referral Network

Networking. You're already an expert. We do it all the time in just about every aspect of our lives. Most of us have asked a friend for a recommendation for a good auto mechanic, a good dentist, a good place to eat. You may even have given your own recommendations to friends and family on a variety of different subjects. Some recommendations work out; others don't. But after awhile, you have a pretty good list of the best places to go or the best people to turn to for a number of different services.

The same is true in the area of professional referrals. You probably know your community and its services better than you think you do. As you take a moment to think about it, you may already know a trusted professional you could speak with, learn from, and/or refer to. Typically, one good professional knows others, so networking beginning with one professional you know by reputation or in a professional capacity may be all you need to start accumulating your file of professional resources.

When you start the networking process, there are a few things you will want to know before making the referral. *First, before you ever pick up the phone to speak with a potential referral source, you will want to have a signed release of information from your client if you plan to talk about things specific to that client.* This is very simply a basic tenet of ethical practice and the law in much of the United States.

Once that is done, you can begin finding out other important information. With all referred professionals, you will want to ask about their training and experience, practice orientation (such as Cognitive Behavior Therapy, psychodynamic, behavior therapy), how long they have been in practice in the area of alcohol use disorder treatment, what certifications and/or licenses they hold (Certified Addictions Counselor, licensed psychologist, licensed physician), what insurances they accept, and whether their practice is open for new clients. You will want to do this during your first contact with the professional because the answers will help guide you in the process of matching client to professional, which we will address a bit later.

If there is no one in the community that you currently know who treats clients with alcohol problems, there are numerous other sources to turn to. The American Society of Addiction Medicine (ASAM) offers physician referrals by specialty and, conveniently, by zip code on its Web page (www.asam.org). Many state psychological associations also offer this service on their Web pages, making it possible to find psychologists who specialize in or are otherwise knowledgeable about alcohol use problems. Additionally, most states have organizations that certify and track individuals who have taken training and passed examinations to become Certified Addictions Counselors (CAC). Many of these organizations also have a Web presence or can be located through the reference desk at public libraries.

Also many counties and/or cities have Information and Referral agencies that are well equipped to make suggestions for possible referrals to agencies and organizations that offer assessment and treatment. Your local Mental Health Association or the United Way also may be able to help you begin to find professionals or organizations in your area. Most telephone books have Human Services sections organized by topic and subtopic. For example: treatment for individuals with alcohol problems, information on the topic of alcohol abuse and dependence, support for family members and friends, and activist organizations are often listed. These ideas are simply to get you started. For some of you it will be enough. Others may want and need additional information.

In addition to scanning local resources, you can access a number of treatment program directories on the Internet. In Appendix A we review and present a variety of treatment directories that are currently available, along with a series of important questions to ask of programs to which you may be thinking of referring a client.

Most states and provinces allow access to databases of professionals who have been censured or disciplined or had their licenses revoked by their particular licensing body. You will always want to check these databases to make certain the professionals you're considering are in good standing with their state or province, as well as their professional association.

The "Match" Game: How to Select the Right Professional

The right fit is important in most areas of people's lives. You wouldn't tolerate a pair of poor-fitting shoes . . . at least not for long! This, of course, is a simplistic example, but the analogy is a good one: You are unlikely to wear a pair of shoes that made you uncomfortable. You probably would take them off quickly and perhaps even throw them away. The same is true for most clients who are considering treatment possibilities for alcohol use problems. They are unlikely to tolerate a professional who isn't

> "Different strokes for different folks."
>
> —SYLVESTER (SLY) STONE

a good match for them. They are not likely to stay in treatment or pursue their treatment goals and may even postpone seeking treatment. Obviously, the right match is important.

The Role of Medical Personnel

There are multiple things to consider when making a match between client and professional. Perhaps the most basic and important is the client's medical status, including mental health. Long-term, heavy drinkers may need medical supervision if they intend to withdraw from alcohol. They also may need to be checked for numerous physical problems that can arise from long-term, heavy use of alcohol, as well as evaluation for co-occurring mental health problems such as depression. Even individuals who meet the definition of "moderate" drinker (no more than 14 drinks a week or 4 drinks at a sitting for men, and no more than 9 drinks a week or 3 drinks at a sitting for women) may need a physical check-up before proceeding with treatment in order to rule out physiological problems. All of these variables will affect a clients' ability to enter and become involved in treatment.

Medical personnel also can be good at identifying individuals with alcohol use problems. Many primary care practitioners make a regular practice of asking their patients about drug and alcohol use. The CAGE screener (see Chapter 4) is free and in the public domain, and is often useful in this context.

The Client with Mental Health and Alcohol Use Problems

For the individual with a co-occurring mental health problem, the proper match is critical. It is beyond the scope of this chapter to go into a discussion of the "chicken and egg" phenomenon (which came first, the mental health problem or the problem with alcohol), neither is it necessary. Most professionals today agree that it is mandatory to evaluate and treat both problems concurrently, and you will want to find a professional who has expertise in both areas.

Individuals with mental health disorders commonly have co-occurring (often referred to as "comorbid") problems with alcohol. The term that professionals use for comorbid mental health and alcohol or substance use problems is "dual diagnosis." In 1990, the National Institute of Mental Health published a study that cited comorbid alcohol problems in 46.2% of people with Bipolar I Disorder (perhaps the most severe form of the disease) and in 39.2% of people with Bipolar II Disorder. The same study reported that 12.2% of people with alcohol dependence (see Chapter 1 for a definition) also have comorbid anxiety disorders. Other studies have suggested that the incidence of comorbidity with anxiety disorders is significantly higher. In 2002, researchers Robert Drake and Kim T. Mueser found that alcohol use disorders are the most common co-occurring disorders in people diagnosed with schizophrenia. Depression, too, is both a reason people turn to alcohol and a complicating factor. Alcohol is a central nervous system depressant, so it can significantly worsen depression. Additionally, alcohol interferes with normal sleep. Although it induces sleep, it interferes with normal sleep stages, causing clients to have very poor sleep. Poor sleep is a contributing factor not only to depression but also to the Bipolar Disorders, and can exacerbate other physiological problems such as musculoskeletal disorders that have pain as one of their symptoms. Clearly, mental health issues are a major factor to consider when making a referral.

Finding Out about the Professional's Style and Method of Practice

After consideration of physical and mental health in matching a client, it's important to know more about the professional to whom you want to make a referral. You'll want to determine the professional's style. Does he or she tend to be confrontational or collaborative, and which style do you think will be a "fit" for the client? Historically, more than a few alcohol and substance treatment programs have been confrontational, urging clients to "get real" or "own your stuff," and even being what might today be considered verbally abusive or disparaging to the client. More modern approaches, spearheaded by the likes of G. Alan Marlatt, William R. Miller, and Stephen Rollnick, have demonstrated the importance and success of collaboration with and positive regard for the client. These methods usually focus on helping clients by using specific guided questioning (sometimes referred to as Socratic questioning because this type of questioning was a part of Socrates' teaching method) to begin to understand the impact of alcohol on their lives and the lives of others, and to determine what, if anything, they'd like to do about it.

You will probably want to ask the professional what addiction model they follow. Do they believe alcohol abuse or dependence is a disease? Genetically

A Socratic Questioning Primer

While it is beyond the scope of this book to give a thorough presentation of this technique, it is likely to be helpful to you to know a little more about Socratic questioning. Socrates, the early Greek philosopher and teacher, presented material to his pupils by asking them questions that stimulated them to think deeply about the topic they were discussing. The questions were contemplative, rigorous, and prompted thought-provoking dialogue between class members and teacher. This same method is now widely used in many therapies—indeed, it is a hallmark of Cognitive Behavior Therapy—and also has been brought to the treatment of persons with alcohol use disorders. Socratic questions are open-ended, that is they cannot usually be answered with a one-word answer or "yes" or "no." Example of a closed question: "Is drinking a problem for you?" Example of a Socratic question: "What evidence is there to support your idea that drinking is a problem for you?" The Socratic question prompts deeper thinking, and can foster collaboration and dialogue between client and therapist.

inevitable? Has a genetic component but can be treated? Must be treated or there is no chance of recovery? Must be treated because there is no way clients can cure themselves? Each answer will affect how the professional regards the client and what type of treatment he or she offers.

Other factors in the "match game" to consider:

- gender
- age
- culture
- race
- religious affiliation
- sexual orientation

Let's consider these in more depth. The gender issue is pretty commonsensical and basic. If the client has a preference—and this should always be ascertained—then it must be considered. Gender dynamics are well documented in the research literature and clearly have an impact on the therapeutic relationship. Remember, without a good therapeutic relationship between client and professional, not much gets done. Even if you believe the client would be better off seeing a professional of a particular gender, that issue may not be as important as getting the client to a competent professional with whom the client can make a good therapeutic connection.

Referrals for Adolescents

Age is another important issue. If the client you are hoping to refer is an adolescent, it will be important to find a professional who specializes in, understands, and has experience in treating adolescents. Adolescents are in the process of widespread development and therefore are in critical cognitive, emotional, and physical developmental stages that will affect how they accept, participate in, and benefit from treatment. Recent research has shown that a critical part of the brain that handles executive functions such as reasoning, judgment, and planning may not be fully developed until around the age of 25. The adolescent with an alcohol problem will not be thinking about it the same way as an adult. This has direct treatment implications.

Also, with an adolescent, you likely will be working with parents, guardians, or other family members to secure treatment. Family members are also likely to be involved in the treatment process itself. It is important that the adolescent feel that he or she is being heard about treatment decisions. A collaborative approach in this instance is important, and you will probably want to avoid making a referral to a professional who has a dogmatic take-it-or-leave-it approach. Depending upon the laws of your state or province, an adolescent of a certain age can request and receive treatment without his or her parent's knowledge. This may be as young as 14. It is always important when working with an adolescent to help him or her understand how his or her parents can be helpful in treatment and recovery, but, depending upon the specific rules of your state or province, the final decision about whether or not to tell parents or guardians may lie with the adolescent. This is often a source of great frustration and concern to parents because they may know or suspect that their son or daughter is in treatment. They may call and demand information. It takes tact and patience to handle these situations. For instance, professionals in this situation might tell a parent that they cannot give out any information but will listen to anything the parent has to say.

Referrals for Older Persons

For the older individual who may be interested in seeking treatment for alcohol-related problems, the referral match is just as important as it is with adolescents. The professional must be knowledgeable and guard against falling into an ageist view of older individuals.

Even though the use of alcohol typically declines as people age, older individuals can and do have problems. Richard D. Blondell, writing in the *Journal of Elder Abuse and Neglect*, suggests that "Approximately 1% to 3% of elderly in the United States suffer from the consequences of excessive alcohol consumption. Many more drink amounts of alcohol that place them at risk for alcohol-related problems." These problems may include falling, motor vehicle accidents if the client is still driving, pedestrian accidents, and relationship problems. Researchers Pilar Sanjuan and James Langenbucher, writing in *Addictions, A Comprehensive Guidebook*, suggest that the incidence of alcohol abuse and dependence in the elderly may be even higher. The attitudes of family, friends, and therapists toward the older individual will have a significant impact on the individual's willingness to evaluate the issue of his or her alcohol use and any problems related to it.

Checklist for Working with Older Individuals

- Will they have to climb stairs to get to your office or within your office?
- Are the chairs in your waiting room tall enough to make it easy to get in and out?
- Do you have wide-bodied pens for easy gripping when filling out forms?
- Are your forms printed in dark, clear type for easy reading?
- Is your office on a bus line for clients who do not drive?
- Has your office staff had training to better deal with older individuals, for example, addressing them by "Mr." or "Mrs." instead of their first names, speaking clearly and distinctly (but not necessarily loudly)?
- Scheduling enough time so that the older client does not feel rushed?

Therapists who consistently work with older clients understand that there are very practical issues to be considered. For example, where is the office of the professional located? Is it easily accessible? Up a flight of stairs? On a bus route? Are chairs in the office high enough and equipped with arms to allow older adults to get in and out of them comfortably? Older adults often require more time for sessions. Rushing jeopardizes the therapeutic relationship. Does the professional to whom you are thinking of referring an older individual have enough time for these clients? Older adults also may have physical problems such as hearing loss that will affect treatment. It is likely that a professional who treats older adults will need permission from the individual to be in close communication with his or her primary care physician and support system. The professional will have to be sensitive to the stressors that older adults face such as loss of job, loss of spouse or partner, caretaking of family or friends, and the possibility of problems with thinking, memory, or other limitations.

Diversity and Referrals

A client's culture has a significant impact on the choice of professional. We are an amazingly diverse nation. In 1992, the United States Census Bureau projected that sometime between the years 2030 and 2050, people of color will make up a statistical majority of the population. Currently, just under half of the student population in public schools are children of color. Cultural considerations in the referral process are obviously important.

A determination of whether the client requires a professional who is fluent in the client's primary language is essential, but other considerations are also important. In many cultures, the family is very important in treatment.

> "To be tested is good. The challenged life may be the best therapist."
>
> —GAIL SHEEHY

In some instances, treatment may not go forward unless the family is consulted and involved. The professional has to be sensitive to aspects of the culture that may be important to the client, such as alternative culture-bound methods for coping with problems.

As it is for culture, so it is for race. You will want to try to determine the racial competence and sensitivity of any professional to whom you refer a client. This may mean asking if they have formal training in cultural and racial competencies or ascertaining the professional's years of experience with a particular race. It may also mean attempting to determine what stage of racial identity the client is in. For example, researchers Derald Wing Sue and David Sue suggest that African-American clients may range from individuals who have a Eurocentric view and would have little difficulty accepting a therapist of the majority culture to individuals who would develop a better therapeutic relationship with a professional of the same race. The best advice is simply to ask the client's preference and be sensitive to his or her needs.

Spirituality and Religion in the Referral Process

Not all that long ago, religious orientation was rarely identified in treatment and even more rarely utilized. Indeed, sometimes it was disparaged and dismissed as unimportant. Now, it is expected that a professional will use what is referred to as the "biopsychosocialspiritual model" of evaluating and treating a client. That's a mouthful, but what it means is that all aspects of a client's life are important to assess and to use when considering making a referral: the biological or physiological (including genetic aspects); the psychological; the social environment, including stressors; and the importance of spiritual or religious beliefs. The individual who professes no religious or spiritual beliefs is unlikely to make a good connection with professionals who characterize themselves a having a strong and particular spiritual or religious orientation. Conversely, the client with strong religious beliefs may not make a connection with a professional who openly professes none. Then again, there are professionals with strong beliefs who do an excellent job of making a connection with clients.

Clients' Sexual Orientation and the Referral Process

The sexual orientation of a client is very important to consider when making a referral. According to the National Gay and Lesbian Taskforce, homophobia is currently a factor in everything from careers to family issues such as marriage and adoption, to medical care. Before thinking about a referral for a gay, lesbian, bisexual, or transgendered client, you should assess your own level of comfort with this population. Can you consider what is in the client's best interests regarding his/her alcohol treatment without the interference of your own thoughts and feelings about their sexual orientation? Will the professional you are considering for a referral do the same? What are the client's thoughts and feelings on this issue?

SELF IMPROVEMENT TECHNIQUE

Quick Check—Referrals

1. You have a client who is asking for a referral to a professional. She is a 46-year-old, married Hispanic woman from a very traditional Catholic family. What are the factors you will want to consider when making a referral? (*Answer: Among the factors you would consider are the importance of her faith, how involved she would like her family to be, and what her level of acculturation is.*)

2. A friend of yours is a high school teacher. She tells you that she has a 16-year-old student who she thinks has a drinking problem. She wants you to talk to the student and perhaps make a referral. Who would you want to consult about this? What factors would you want to consider if you should choose to make a referral? If you decide to meet with the student, should you inform his or her parent or guardian? (*Answer: Unless you are employed by your friend's school as a school psychologist or guidance counselor or other similar professional, and your friend is making a formal referral, your best bet is to suggest that your friend consult the guidance or other counselors available in her school.*)

We've covered a few of the issues relating to matching a client to a professional. It may seem overwhelming, but if you have established a good alliance with your client and you have some good background information about the professional to whom you're thinking of making the referral then you are well on your way. Additionally, you can also talk with the client about this, saying that you are making the best referral you know at this time, but urge him or her to evaluate the professional for his or her ability to work collaboratively to decide if there is a problem and how it might be addressed.

The Suicidal or Homicidal Client: Protection and Duty to Warn

The client who is in jeopardy of harming self or others can be difficult and frightening even to professionals who are familiar with these kinds of situations. When working with her clients, one of the co-authors makes a regular check of their level of suicidal and homicidal thinking. She makes it a point to develop a close, collaborative relationship with clients such that they tend to let her know what's going on with them before she asks. However, that cannot always be relied upon, so at the very first session it is important to say to the client, "When people are going through tough times, especially when they're thinking about trying to do something about a drinking problem, sometimes they feel as if they cannot be safe, or they may feel like harming someone else. Have you ever felt like that? Do you feel like that now? As we work together, I will make it a point to check with you regularly about this."

Referral

Most of the do's and don'ts of making referrals involve something you already have and use: common sense. For example, it is clear that confidentiality in any treatment or referral setting is primary, although there are limits. For example, if clients have indicated that they cannot remain safe and have thoughts and intentions of harming themselves or others, confidentiality no longer exists. Laws vary from state to state and country to country, so it will be important to have an understanding of these laws.

The Health Insurance Portability and Accountability Act (HIPAA) requirements apply in all medical and many other treatment settings that utilize electronic communications such as fax machines to communicate information. Protecting confidentiality means everything from securing files (computer and paper) to not discussing client cases in areas where this information can be overheard, to not leaving voice mail messages with any identifying information unless specifically given written permission (usually called a Release of Information) to do so. For example, in leaving a voice mail message you would NOT want to say, "Hi, this is Mary Jones. I'd like to refer Sam Smith to you for assessment of his drinking problem." You may not wish to leave a voice mail message at all; however, if you do leave a message, you will still have to follow-up regularly to make sure you get in touch with the professional to whom you wish to refer. Referrals should always be made as promptly as possible.

Other do's and don'ts of referrals:

- When calling a professional to whom you wish to refer, do identify yourself completely (name, title, telephone number), and, if leaving a message, do specify when it's best to get a hold of you ("I can be reached on Mondays from 1 to 5 p.m."). Also let them know whether it's urgent that they reply in a specified time: "Please call me before the close of business today to let me know if you are accepting referrals." If you do not have a response by that time or shortly thereafter, it will be important for you to contact another professional. This doesn't mean that the first professional you contacted cannot be a resource in the future.

- Do find out if there is specific paperwork required in making a referral, how to get copies of the required forms, and to whom you can talk if you have questions about completing the paperwork.

- Do find out from clients what insurances they have and whether their coverage allows them to be referred to the professional you have chosen. Many insurance companies have specific lists of professionals to whom they refer their policyholders.

- *Do NOT make a referral to a professional in an emergency situation.* If the client is in jeopardy of harming him/herself or someone else, you must call 911, Crisis Intervention, or another similar service and make appropriate arrangements. Never leave a client alone in an emergency situation. Always wait with them until emergency services arrive. Generally, it is not a good idea to transport the client yourself or allow a family member or friend to do so as legal problems may result.

It will be important to assess the following:

- Is there suicidal ideation? In other words, is the client currently thinking about self harm?
- Is it just a passing thought ("Sometimes I think it would really be nice not to wake up in the morning.") or is it a thought with a plan ("Things are getting too hard for me. I've been thinking that it would be really easy just to drive my car off a bridge.").
- Ask the client if he or she has ever had a previous suicide attempt. Clients who have had suicide attempts before are at significantly greater risk for additional attempts. This is especially true for males. Additionally, ask the client if any close family members or friends have ever attempted or completed suicide. This is an important question because it will tell you if the client's social support system has, in essence, given tacit approval to this dangerous behavior.

What if you have a client who has expressed a wish to harm someone else? What do you do? This is usually referred to as the "duty to warn." And this is a difficult issue because laws differ widely. *It will be very important to check with your state or province about the specific laws with regard to duty to warn.* Some laws require that the client have a specific person in mind, and, in some jurisdictions, a time frame before there is a duty to warn. For example, "That jerk of a boss of mine just fired me because he thinks I've relapsed, although he told me it was because I wasn't doing my job right. You know, he's always been on my case. I think I'll just go up there after he gets off of work tonight and beat the heck out of him. That'll teach him!" In this instance, it will be important first to help the client calm down ("You usually have good judgment when you're calm. How about taking a moment to relax a bit, and then we can think this through together?"). If the client is still angry enough to want to harm the other person, it will be important to tell the client, "You know we can't let that happen to him or to you. What do you think is the best way to protect both of you?" If the client is unable to reason through this situation, you will want to consider breaching confidentiality to warn the other person and even to consider seeking help in getting the client into a hospital setting or calling police or emergency services. *Again, always check the laws of your particular state or province.*

Helping the Client to Consider Treatment . . . or Motivation, Motivation, Motivation

It's not possible to motivate someone who isn't motivated, right? You just have to wait until they come around to your way of thinking. Or, they have to hit bottom before they accept the idea that they need treatment. We've all heard that. Interestingly, it's not true. It's quite possible to help clients begin to consider the effect of alcohol use on their lives even during your first meeting with them.

You may have heard the term "resistance." You've probably heard that's what everyone who has an alcohol problem and is in "denial" does. You know they've got a problem. They don't think they have a problem. Voila, "resistance." But, actually, resistance isn't a bad thing at all. Reframed, it's one way clients can tell you that they disagree with you and it's probably going to be useful to take a different path to help them consider how alcohol factors into their lives.

Before even sitting down with clients, put yourself in their place. What would it feel like to you if you weren't even thinking that you had a problem and someone came to you and said, "You're an alcoholic, you're in denial, and you have to get treatment." Do you think your response would be, "Why of COURSE! Let's get started!" Unlikely. You would probably be surprised, angry, resentful, and maybe all three. You likely would begin to defend your position: "I'm fine. I don't have a problem. I can hold my liquor and I could quit any time I wanted to. But I don't need to quit. And just who are you anyway? This is MY business!"

Are you getting the idea that labels aren't particularly useful and can really rupture any sort of alliance you may have established with the client? Are you also getting the idea that labels for behavior such as "resistance" and "denial" also aren't particularly useful? Then, you're on the right path to helping clients consider their alcohol use, whether it may be problematic, and what, if anything, they'd like to do about it.

Authors and researchers William Miller and Stephen Rollnick have developed a technique for helping clients enhance their motivation for treatment. They call it "Motivational Interviewing," and it has several aspects. When working with clients to enhance their acceptance of professional help:

- *Express empathy*. Interestingly, acceptance and empathy reduce resistance significantly. The confrontational techniques of the past have not proven to work as well as empathy.

- *Develop discrepancy*. This helps clients become more aware of how their alcohol use has had an impact on their lives and, perhaps, the lives of others. Many clients will bring up an aspect of this themselves. "I'm not an alcoholic. Far from it. But my doctor says these stomach pains I'm having could be due to drinking and I'm wondering about that." You might then respond, "So you're wondering if your drinking is having an adverse impact on your health." Notice that there is no preaching, no labeling? Just a simple reflection of the client's own concerns that allows the client to continue to think about this idea without becoming defensive.

- *Avoid arguing*. If you argue that clients are alcoholic or even say, "You have a problem," they are likely to dig in and defend their positions. You are unlikely, in this case, to develop discrepancy. They will defend their position and it will be difficult, if not impossible, to find and enhance motivation.

- *Roll with resistance.* When the client says, "I don't have a drinking problem!" don't counter with, "Oh, yes you do! Everyone knows it but you!" Think of resistance as an opportunity to gently and empathically explore the idea further.

If the client is willing, this may also be an opportunity to use a technique called "cost/benefit analysis" to help the client think about alcohol use problems and the idea of treatment. This technique explores the advantages and disadvantages of various positions. For example, you would ask the client to list on a piece of paper the advantages to continuing to drink (tastes good, makes me relax, helps me socialize, etc.). Then, ask about any disadvantages. Don't put words in the client's mouth. Allow him or her to create this list. You can, however, mention items that the client may have said before. "I'm recalling that you said you were concerned about what your doctor had said about your stomach pains. Would you consider that a disadvantage?" Once that is complete, you then turn it around and ask the client to list the disadvantages to modifying their alcohol use (too hard, not sure they can do it, would lose social group). Finally, ask the client to list the advantages to modifying their use. Ask the client what he or she makes of these lists and then listen. Allow the client to think aloud about this. At the conclusion of this exercise, the client may have concluded that it would be useful to consult a professional to explore the idea of modifying his or her alcohol use.

Crises

Crisis. Just the word can be frightening. It may evoke thoughts of police, firemen, accidents, emotional pain, and physical jeopardy. The word "crisis" comes from the Greek word for "decision" and clearly, we are making all sorts of decisions in crisis situations. But before you think about making decisions *during* a crisis, let's think about crises *before* they arise, because prevention is the best way to deal with a crisis.

Many professionals find it useful to address the possibility of crisis situations with a client before one occurs. This is actually something you probably do all the time in your own life. For example, you probably have an idea of what you would do if a water pipe breaks in your home: Find the closest water shut off point, protect items from becoming wet, call a plumber, or, if you're skilled in such things, repair it yourself. You know what to do in case of that kind of emergency situation.

The same is true in working with a client. When things are calm ask the client, "How would you like to handle things if you (relapse, feel like hurting yourself or someone else, feel as if you're losing control, etc.)?" Then, you and the client can list potential crisis situations and the desired solutions. This allows time for discussion and deliberation and often results in the client feeling in control and prepared. It also encourages proactive thinking and behavior, as well as promoting a sense of collaboration between you and the client. A copy of this list (see Table 3.1) is given to the client, complete with phone numbers or other emergency contact information, and kept with the client at all times. The original should be kept by you in a place where you can access and refer to it if you need to.

So, what do you do if you haven't had time to plan ahead with the client, or this person is new to you, or for some other reason a crisis occurs? Remember the importance of having a good alliance with the client? This becomes very important in preventing or dealing with a crisis situation. Trust goes a long way toward averting or alleviating crisis situations. When a client trusts you or simply feels comfortable with you, it becomes significantly easier to halt or prevent a crisis.

So, just how do you build a good alliance even during a crisis? What if you've never met this person before? What if you're a family member and there may have been a few bumps in the relationship road? Three things help build a good alliance:

- active listening,
- reflection,
- empathy

Let's take a look at these three things in more depth. Active listening means focusing your full attention on the person you're listening to. Don't formulate responses. Don't think about what you're going to say. Just listen. Allow the client to talk as long as he or she would like, as long as they remain safe. Minimize interruptions. Turn off cell phones or put them on mute. Avoid taking other calls. Minimize distractions. Avoid any other activities except focused listening.

Then, when it's appropriate, reflect back to the client what he or she has said. Reflection means letting someone know that you have accurately heard them and

Table 3.1: Sample Crisis Plan.

Situation	Plan of Action
1. My wife is nagging me.	Take a time out, use my relaxation techniques, call my friend, tell my wife I need a break, but I will come back to finish the discussion.
2. I had a long day and want to use.	Go to a meeting, call a friend, get out and get some exercise.
3. Depressed and thinking about self harm.	Call a therapist, call a friend, call Crisis Intervention (list phone number).

giving them an opportunity to correct your impression, if necessary. For example, "Lynn, I hear you saying that you got a DUI (driving under the influence) citation. You think your husband will leave you because of this and that really worries you. You wonder if you can stay safe. Is this right?" Or, "Okay, if I'm getting what you're saying, you believe that you can't do anything about losing your job and you wonder if you can stay sober." Allow the client to continue talking. Many times just the simple act of talking and being heard will defuse a crisis.

Empathy is always an important aspect of coping with or preventing crises. Empathy means asking yourself to try to experience the feelings and thoughts of another person even when the person cannot fully communicate them. The person to whom empathy is expressed feels accepted and understood.

When a Crisis Is in Progress

Taken together, active listening, reflection, and empathy are powerful tools in helping to prevent or resolve crisis situations. But even when there is a good, trusting alliance, crises can and do happen. When a crisis situation occurs, it is important to address it quickly. As mentioned earlier, in the instance of a threatened suicide, it is critical to ensure the client's safety. There is a widespread belief that if you ask someone if they are thinking of harming themselves, it will force their hand. This is myth. You *must* assess whether someone is suicidal in order to get them the appropriate help, and there are numerous ways to do this. You can ask them, "Are you thinking of harming yourself?" "Are you having trouble staying safe right now?" "Are you having thoughts about killing yourself?" Most clients are relieved to have this out in the open and will respond honestly.

When a client cannot guarantee his or her safety, it is important to call 911 or Crisis Intervention or whatever organization in your city, state, or province handles emergency situations. If possible, ask the client to make the call as you stand by to support and to assist if necessary. Helping the client to feel that he or she is in control during a situation that feels so out of control can help to defuse the situation and promote self-help behaviors. As has been said before, never leave a client alone in this kind of emergency situation. If possible, bring another person into the room with you, provided the person remains calm and does not exacerbate the situation. That individual can remain with the client if you have to answer a phone call regarding the emergency.

When emergency personnel arrive, you should explain that he or she is having difficulty remaining safe and gently ask the client to describe what has been going on. Most emergency personnel have dealt with this kind of situation many times and are quite good at making certain that things stay calm and helping to get the client to the emergency room. You can ask the client if he or she would like you to accompany them, but understand that this is not always allowed. You will want to ask the client if you can contact friends or family members for them. (Be sure to note in writing that the client gave you verbal permission to contact certain specified individuals.)

The Dangerous Situation

A threat to a client's safety may not always be from the client. Another individual may come to your location with the intention of harming your client or you. In these circumstances, you should follow your agency guidelines, and you must call emergency personnel immediately. If there are other personnel at your location, enlist their help. If you sense that the other individual intends harm, stay in or proceed to the most public area of your location and call emergency services.

Another crisis situation that can occur is when the client becomes angry and physically aggressive. This is more likely when the client comes to your office and you find that he or she has been drinking, or if the client has a mental health diagnosis and also has been drinking. The basic steps to take include the following:

- Make sure that you are not alone with the client. In an office setting, that may mean arranging for office personnel to remain with you or alerting personnel to the possibility that the client may be angry and aggressive.
- Give the client physical space. Never crowd someone who is angry.
- Never touch the client. It is rarely wise to come into physical contact of any kind with a client (other than a handshake when first meeting), but this is especially true when a client is angry.
- If necessary, allow the client to leave, and call emergency services if you believe that he or she cannot remain safe. As we said before, each state or province will have its own requirements about your responsibilities to a client, so it will be important to know these ahead of time.

If a client is merely angry and not physically aggressive, allow the client to talk. If there are other people within earshot and the client is very loud, quietly say, "I want to listen, but our conversation isn't confidential right now. And I'm also concerned about the other people in this building." Talking very quietly is a good technique for getting people to listen, even when they're angry. Almost invariably, they stop shouting so that they can hear what you're saying. They may remain angry, but they're listening. Once this is accomplished, you can allow the client to talk and then implement the three techniques previously outlined: active listening, reflection, and empathy.

Any crisis situation must be followed up with a plan for longer-term treatment. If the client has been admitted to the hospital, it is likely that hospital personnel (psychiatrists, psychologists, therapists, and social workers) will be involved in arranging treatment following discharge. If the client gives permission for you to be involved, you can work with this group of professionals to make referrals for the client after he or she is stable and has been discharged.

Involving Friends and Family

In the best of all possible worlds, families of clients attempting to cope with alcohol use disorders would be supportive, caring, limit setting, attentive, and actively involved. They wouldn't nag, criticize, over-protect, deny, or challenge inappropriately. They wouldn't have alcohol use problems themselves. There are families such as this, but they are rare in any setting, not just in the setting of alcohol treatment. Remember, most of the individuals with alcohol use problems find a way to quit or modify on their own, so the persons who are seen in treatment are those for whom this has not yet been possible. Their families have been along for the ride or, perhaps, even been actively involved in the maintenance of problems.

Research by Timothy O'Farrell and William Fals-Stewart has shown that family involvement can be useful not only for the client but for the family as well. Family involvement can increase ability to cope, reduce domestic violence and social costs, as well as decrease emotional problems in the children of individuals with alcohol problems.

So, what do you do about family (and friend) involvement? First, consider the age of the client. If the client is an adolescent, the family by law may be involved. In some states and provinces, adolescents of a certain age can decide for themselves to enter treatment and whether to have family members involved. Be sure to know the laws and/or regulations of your jurisdiction.

Second, get to know the client and his or her family and friends, if possible. You are likely to be required to have written permission from the client to do so. This request can be couched in overall treatment concerns for the client. "I know you've told me that you think your family is pretty angry right now because of your DUI citation, but I've found that family involvement can really be a help when trying to decide how to deal with alcohol problems."

Third, determine if there are any family members with alcohol use or dependence problems. It will be very difficult for the client to modify or eliminate his or her alcohol use if there are active drinkers in the family. While it may not be possible to get family members to stop drinking, it may be possible to ask them to engage in harm reduction, such as removing alcohol from the environment and not drinking in front of the client. Many family members who are willing to do this because of their concern for the client find that during the client's treatment they have begun to address their own alcohol use problems.

Fourth, be alert for family dynamic problems. For example, most professionals are aware of the "identified patient" problem. This is where the individual with alcohol use problems is the focus of family attention and dynamics. There may be other family problems—even significant problems such as abuse or marital issues—but these have been camouflaged by the client's problems. As the client begins to take control of his or her alcohol use problems, these other issues become apparent and need to be addressed. Many professionals have noted that if these other problems are not addressed, the client may begin using alcohol again because he or she is unable to cope with the family distress that has emerged from his or her sobriety.

Fifth, set clear boundaries in working with the client and his or her family. For example, discourage "tattletales." Treatment requires the client to understand his or her own problems with regard to alcohol use and to take control of his or her own recovery. When family members "tell on" the client, it encourages a defensive posture and decreases the collaboration of a good alliance.

As noted in the segment about culture, for some clients family will be a very important part of treatment, and treatment may not be initiated or go forward without family involvement. Indeed, in some extreme cases, the patriarch of a family will be the individual with whom you begin working first. This is unusual in the typical dynamic of American culture, which focuses on the individual, but you will need to be sensitive to this if you encounter a family with this ethic. Forcing American individualism on a family such as this will almost assuredly end treatment.

Risk Management Strategies

Risk management is inherent in everything we do. If you live in cold climates, you reduce the risk of having an accident while driving or becoming stuck in snow by ensuring that your vehicle has good snow tires and fresh antifreeze, that you have a cell phone or other way to call for help, and perhaps even blankets in the car. Or consider your health. You manage the potential risk of having a heart attack by not smoking, watching your diet, taking medication if needed, and exercising. You may be especially sensitive to risk management if you have family members with heart disease.

Risk Management: Protection for You and Your Client

There are two aspects of risk management when working with clients with alcohol use problems: protecting them and protecting you. As we mentioned earlier in this chapter, crisis prevention can be addressed ahead of the occurrence of a potential risk by talking with your client about it. For example, you will likely want to address the risk of relapse. This would include assessing how long the client has been able to appropriately manage his or her alcohol use. If the client has opted for sobriety, how many days, weeks, or months has he or she been sober? What kind of support system does the client have that can assist if relapse occurs or seems as if it might occur? What are the signs of imminent relapse, such as Driving by the bar or club where the client used to drink, Drinking soda or other non-alcoholic beverage in a bar with old drinking buddies, Spending a great deal of time remembering pleasant times associated with drinking. You and the client collaboratively will want to make a list of potential risks and decide ahead of time how these will be addressed.

The same will be true of other risks. Ask the client to brainstorm potential risks with you and how he or she would like to deal with them.

Managing risk for you concerns a number of different areas. One of the most fundamental is financial and legal protection. Do you have malpractice insurance?

Does your agency or workplace? How are these kinds of situations handled? Do you have someone (a professional from your networking list, for example) with whom you can consult if you have problems or questions? And, *always* be certain to document your observations, concerns, and the work you have done with the client. Also be certain to document your consultations with other professionals, *as well as the fact that you had a Release of Information from your client to do so.*

Your physical risk management entails your physical safety. First, think about how to arrange your office. If you are physically threatened, can you get out of the room easily? Does anything—such as a desk or other furniture—block your way? Is your office equipped with a "panic button?" Are you a solo practitioner? If so, you will want your office personnel to have a clear understanding about what to do if a client becomes problematic. Just as you have brainstormed risk situations with the client, you will want to do the same thing for yourself. Consult with professionals and ask their opinions about what entails "risk management" for you, then put in place the measures required.

Referral Follow-Up

So, you've got your list of professionals, you've played "the match game," you've brainstormed problematic areas with the client, and you've managed to help the client find the motivation to seek professional help. Congratulations! This is no small feat, but there is one more aspect to making an appropriate referral and that's follow-up. First, be sure to have written permission from the client to contact the professional to whom you have made the referral. Then, spend some time with the client discussing why it will be important for you to follow-up: appropriate care and concern, making sure that the professional as well as the client have made contact and set up a first appointment, and finding out if there is any assistance you can continue to provide. Besides being professionally appropriate, referral follow-up says to the client that you care and are not just going to "refer and run." You will also get good information about the quality of the professionals to whom you refer, allowing you to make future referrals with confidence.

Key Terms

Comorbid. Occurring together. Example: Clinical depression and alcohol abuse when occurring together are referred to as "comorbid" problems. Individuals with comorbid problems such as depression and alcohol abuse are also referred to as having a "dual diagnosis."

DUI or DWI. Abbreviations for "Driving Under the Influence" or "Driving While Intoxicated." Different states and provinces may use either one when referring to this criminal behavior.

Duty to protect/Duty to warn. Legal terms that refer to a counselor or therapist's obligation to inform someone when the client may be a danger to others. The level of responsibility differs from state to state.

Motivational Interviewing. A method created by William Miller and Stephen Rollnick that can help to motivate clients to think about alcohol use problems. It involves the use of empathic understanding to develop clients' own dissonant thoughts about alcohol use.

Socratic questioning. A method of helping clients to come to their own understanding of problems by asking open-ended questions that create deeper thinking.

Recommended Reading

Some of the books that have been beneficial to many therapists and others who deal with clients with alcohol use problems include *Motivational Interviewing,* by William Miller and Stephen Rollnick (New York: Guilford, 1991); *The Suicide and Homicide Risk Assessment and Prevention Treatment Planner,* by Jack Klott and Arthur E. Jongsma (Hoboken, NJ: Wiley, 2004); *When Psychological Problems Mask Medical Disorders,* by James Morrison (New York: Guilford, 1997); and *Where to Start and What to Ask, An Assessment Handbook,* by Susan Lukas (New York: W. W. Norton, 1993).

TRUTH OR FICTION

QUIZ ANSWERS
1. False   2. False   3. True   4. False   5. False

CHAPTER 4

Assessment and Treatment Planning

After reading this chapter, you will be able to answer true or false to the following statements:

1. Treatment planning is needed basically to satisfy the insurance companies. True or False?

2. Once you've assessed for safety, you don't need to do it again. True or False?

3. A genogram can be a tool for therapy, but it isn't useful for treatment planning. True or False?

4. Treatment planning is a good way to enhance the therapeutic alliance. True or False?

5. The therapist should be the only one to create the treatment plan because he or she is the expert. True or False?

Answers on p. 69.

Treatment Plan as the Map to Success

Let's say you wanted to drive to Chicago. You probably wouldn't set out without a good map, an idea of the road conditions ahead (including tolls or other costs), where you might want to stop along the way, who you wanted to travel with, and a timetable for getting there. If you did, you *might* end up in Chicago, but you might end up someplace else, wondering just how it happened that you didn't get to Chicago.

The same is true for treatment planning. A treatment plan is a road map, if you will, for guiding treatment. Without it, treatment becomes just a variety of techniques cobbled together without direction or cohesion or the possibility of evaluation of its success or failure. You *might* help your client get to his or her goal this way, but you might not. And if you didn't, it would be difficult, if not impossible, to figure out where things went astray.

A treatment plan serves a number of purposes. By starting out with a valid and complete treatment plan, you and the client have a good idea of where you're going and how you're going to get there. But it also serves another, very important purpose: It allows you to stop at any point during treatment to assess how it's going. Are the goals still important? Are you and the client in agreement about whether treatment is effective? Do you need to make changes in the treatment plan to better reflect how things are going?

Treatment planning—or at least the idea of it—has been around for more than four decades, beginning with the medical domain and spreading into mental health and substance abuse treatment about a decade later. Accreditation bodies such as the Joint Commission on Accreditation of Healthcare Organizations first began accrediting general medical hospitals, but now it conducts evaluations of a wide variety of agencies and care organizations, including those involved with the treatment of substance use disorders. Today, in most states and provinces, it is not possible to receive third-party reimbursement without documentation such as treatment planning.

> **"And with the new testing and research that's going on, I see a cure on the horizon."**
>
> —GERALDINE A. FERRARO

The Beginning of It All: The Intake

So, how do you start? You begin with a thorough intake interview. Everything proceeds from this: diagnosis, screening, choice of assessment instruments, and treatment planning.

At a minimum, an intake is a formal procedure for getting the client into the agency or care organization's system. It will identify basic information such as name, address, social security or other identifying number, and date of birth. It also gathers other important information, such as work situation, current and past health problems that may have a bearing on treatment, a history of alcohol use, current legal problems, and any other things the client considers to be problematic. It also will identify any mental health issues in addition to alcohol-use problems, assess risk of self-harm or harm to others, and begin to establish the all-important therapeutic alliance without which very little happens in treatment.

A well-done intake will give you a picture of the client not just as someone with a possible alcohol use disorder but as a person. And you never treat a disorder, you treat a person. Of course, that will include detailed information about alcohol use, but it will also give you a good idea of the individual. How did they do in school? Did they drop out? Did they drop out but go back for a GED (general equivalency diploma)? Were they in the military? What form of discharge do they have? What did they learn? Have they ever been married? How many times? Do they have children? If the children are under age, does the client live with or support the children? Did anyone else in the client's family have alcohol use problems? How were those addressed? What is their ethnic identity, sexual orientation, or religious affiliation? Have they ever been in treatment before? If so, how did it go? What do they remember about their treatment? How many jobs have they held? Which was the longest? Which was the most satisfying?

Additionally, the intake will gather detailed information about alcohol use. When did the client have his or her first drink? What was the reaction? Is there anyone else in the client's extended family who drinks? How much do these individuals drink? Does your client think that these individuals have a drinking problem? What is the frequency of your client's use? What amounts do they consume? Do they have a preferred drink? What problems can the client identify about his or her alcohol use? Has the client ever tried to quit or reduce alcohol use? How many times? What was the longest period of abstinence or moderation? Was there a history of lapses? Relapses? How did the relapse occur? Who was with the client at the time of relapse? What was the setting? What were the identifiable triggers as the client sees them? What other drugs (including caffeine, nicotine, illegal drugs, prescription drugs and any over-the-counter drugs) does the client use on a regular basis?

Some clinicians neglect to ask about over-the-counter drugs. This is a mistake because it is important to know about *all* psychoactive substances the client uses. It will give you a great deal more information if, for example, you know that the client has been using St. John's wort, an herb believed to have antidepressant properties. Knowing this, you can refer the client for an evaluation and possibly treatment of depression, and it will give you insight into the client's use of alcohol. What role did the St. John's wort play? Did the client use it when he or she was drinking? During periods when he or she was abstinent?

The intake will begin to guide you toward thoughts about placement. The American Society of Addiction Medicine (www.asam.org) has suggested placement criteria that take into account withdrawal risk, biomedical conditions, emotional or behavioral complications, recovery environment, treatment acceptance and/or resistance, and relapse potential. From these, levels of care ranging from outpatient to medically managed intensive inpatient emerge. While these criteria may be helpful, you will want to take into consideration much more about the client before thinking about placement.

The Big Picture: The Genogram

You may already know about and use genograms. These diagrams of family organization, problems, health, and relationships are an excellent tool to help the clinician get familiar with the client individually, as well as letting the client appreciate past and current challenges and know about strengths and resources for addressing problems.

In a typical genogram, females are represented by circles, and males by squares. Straight lines connecting a circle and a square usually indicate a marriage, and a dotted line a romantic or physical relationship other than marriage.

Other visual representations indicate how the client views relationships. For example, one straight line between two siblings suggests a cordial, but not warm relationship, where three straight lines would indicate a very strong, perhaps enmeshed, connection. A squiggly line between family members suggests a poor, but civil relationship, where three squiggly lines might indicate open hostility.

Genograms also include information about health. An "x" through a circle or square indicates that the individual is deceased. Notes about health can be jotted down beside a circle or square indicating, for example, that the client's maternal aunt died of cirrhosis after years of alcohol use or that depression runs in the family.

Typically, genograms involve three generations, but even simple ones can be useful.

Figure 4.1 shows a couple who were married for 25 years before the husband died of pancreatic cancer (a risk factor for heavy drinkers) at age 49 and who was a heavy drinker. They had three children: two males and one female. The female is the middle child and she has an older brother and a younger brother. The two male children drink. One is a "social" drinker, and the other is a heavy drinker. The mother and her daughter do not drink at all. The mother has a very close relationship with her daughter but has conflicted relationships (one squiggly line with her "social" drinker son and two squiggly lines with the son who is a heavy drinker) with her other children.

There are a number of things the client might conclude about this genogram. The mother tends to have poor relationships with her children who drink. The son who is a heavy drinker has the poorest relationship with his mother. If the client knows that pancreatic cancer often arises in individuals who have recurrent bouts of pancreatitis (a severe and often life-threatening inflammation of the

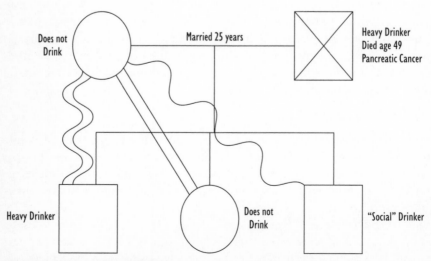

Figure 4.1: A simple genogram.

pancreas—the gland that secrets insulin) and that pancreatitis is often experienced by heavy drinkers, he or she may conclude that the father's heavy drinking contributed to his death from pancreatic cancer.

Genograms can be and usually are much more complex than this one, including multiple generations. Genograms are typically a work in progress. They can be started during intake and can be added to during subsequent meetings with the client.

The genogram is an excellent tool for showing family patterns of drinking, of relationship problems, of health problems, and other problems. Once you have constructed one, it is important to ask the client, "What do you make of this? Do you see any patterns of problems? Any particular strengths?" Clients are often very good at seeing patterns. Using a genogram as part of your intake interview often helps clients begin to think about goals for treatment, what obstacles there are to achieving those goals, and what strengths the client has to accomplish his or her goals.

Insurance

In addition to all of the above, you will certainly want to inquire about insurance coverage, including provisions for treatment, co-pays, limits of coverage, and whether you are an identified provider for that insurance program. If the client has no insurance, you must know your agency's policy about this. Does your agency or care organization have a sliding fee scale? Does your agency accept a certain number of pro bono cases? If so, how are clients evaluated for economic necessity, and is this part of your job or does someone else in your agency take care of this? If your agency or care organization does not provide a sliding fee scale or pro bono services, do state or province laws require you to make a referral? If not, do you have an ethical obligation to do so?

Screening Evaluation or Assessment Battery

As part of an intake you may want to conduct a screening evaluation. A "screener" is obviously not a complete assessment. Rather, it gives a general idea of whether there is a problem and, with some screeners, something about the severity of the problem. In 1974, Demmie Mayfield, Gail McLeod, and Patricia Hall developed the CAGE screener for alcohol problems. This screener is in the public domain, so there is no charge for it. It is brief and can be administered in a few minutes. Clients who answer "yes" to two of the four items on the questionnaire are considered to have a drinking problem. The four items on the CAGE questionnaire are:

1. Have you ever felt you should Cut down on your drinking?
2. Have people Annoyed you by criticizing your drinking?
3. Have you ever felt bad or Guilty about your drinking?
4. Have you ever had a drink first thing in the morning to steady your nerves or get rid of a hangover? (Eye opener)

Pitfalls to Avoid in the Intake Process

- *Not scheduling enough time.* Rushing jeopardizes the therapeutic alliance. Think about it. Would you want your first meeting with a helping professional to be a five-minute "How are you? What's the problem? Take this prescription and see me in six weeks" encounter? Certainly not. A thorough intake takes time, commonly 60–90 minutes. If you are seeing elderly clients, it can take longer than that. Remember, the intake sets the tone for the therapeutic relationship, treatment planning, and the treatment process.
- *Not setting the stage or telling the client how long the intake will take.* If the client comes in thinking that completing paperwork and the intake interview will last about 20 minutes and he or she has to be at work after that, the therapeutic alliance can be at risk. In a phone call several days prior to the intake, tell the client, "We do intakes at our office at 123 Any Street. Do you know that location?" If the client doesn't, provide directions and confirm that the client understands them. Then tell the client, "Be sure to bring your insurance information and a list of any medications you're taking. Intakes usually take about 60-90 minutes. Do you have any questions or concerns?" This gives the client a chance to make changes in plans, if necessary, and sets the stage for a collaborative working relationship.
- *Not helping the client feel as relaxed as possible.* Anyone coming in for an intake regarding their use of alcohol is likely to be more than a little anxious and probably defensive. An anxious or defensive individual is not likely to be candid about the problems that brought them to you in the first place. How would you want to be treated in the same situation? Would you want someone to be very businesslike and crisp, or would you like them to be cordial and welcoming? Depending upon the regulations of your agency or care organization, you may want to offer a cup of coffee or tea, a soda, or simply water. You may want to spend a few moments in "chit chat" about the weather, the traffic, how easy or difficult it was for the client to find your location. This gives the client a chance to relax and, hopefully, to feel comfortable enough to begin the intake and be candid about the information being requested.

Writing in *Addictions, A Comprehensive Guidebook*, Dennis M. Donovan cites several other screeners including the Alcohol Use Disorders Identification Test (AUDIT). Developed in 1991 by the World Health Organization, AUDIT is a validated 10-item questionnaire that takes about two minutes to conduct and is easily hand scored. AUDIT is available in several languages. The manual and forms are available at no-charge; however, there is a fee for a training module. (http://www.who.int/substance_abuse/publications/alcohol/en/).

You may also want to consider giving an assessment battery that will cover a variety of domains, including withdrawal risk, drinking frequency and quantity, motivation for change, severity of dependence, consequences of drinking, co-occurring pathology, coping skills, self-efficacy, and high-risk situations. In choosing one or more assessment instruments to use in evaluating your clients, you should follow these criteria:

1. Brief and easy to administer.
2. Low cost and easy to obtain and score.
3. Written in non-technical language.
4. Easy to interpret and explain to clients.
5. Reliable (measuring consistently) and good at predicting real-world outcome.
6. Sensitive to change.

Rotgers (2002) outlined the importance of tailoring an assessment battery not only to the needs of the client but also to the needs of your agency or care organization. "The assembly of an effective assessment battery always needs to be done with local needs in mind. A practice or agency that treats primarily multi-problem inner city alcohol dependent people who are under significant pressure from welfare or other legal authorities to be completely abstinent will have different assessment requirements than one that focuses, for example, primarily on moderation training with middle class suburbanites."

Okay, now you've gotten a good intake, and you've either done a quick screening of the client or an assessment battery that fits the parameters of your agency or care organization as well as the client (and also have a good idea of how you're going to monitor the success or failure of treatment). You have a very good idea about the client, you have basic information, a good take on his or her alcohol use history, and some perspective on his or her problems with drinking. You have considered appropriate placement. If you have decided that the client is appropriate for outpatient treatment, you may have even had one or two sessions with

> "Thinking well to be wise: planning well, wiser: doing well wisest and best of all."
> —MALCOLM FORBES

him or her. (Many agencies or care organizations do not require a treatment plan until the second or third session to allow for the collection of information, the development of the therapeutic alliance, and time for the client to think about relevant goals.)

THINGS TO REMEMBER

Before you administer individual assessments or assessment batteries, be sure that you have been trained in their administration, scoring, and especially, their interpretation.

So, how about that treatment plan? Your agency or care organization already may have a form for treatment planning, but there are still the important steps of logically defining the problem, collaborating on the goals, and planning the treatment steps. Even with the guidance of a form, you will still have a number of things to think about:

- Specifically, what is the problem? The "specific" part is important. It is not possible to plan treatment for "becoming a better person" or "being happy." In the latter instance, what would "happy" look like? What would the client be doing, thinking, or feeling if he or she were "happy?" In the treatment of alcohol use disorders, what are the specific problems? Too many DUIs? Being late for work? Relationship problems? Physical problems as a result of drinking? This will guide you and the client toward setting a goal that can be accomplished.
- Specifically, which problem are you and the client going to address? There may be many problem areas, but collaboratively identifying the most important is a first step. If the problem is being late to work as a result of drinking, the specific problem to be addressed may be, "Being on time for work every day."
- What are the steps needed to address the problem and move toward the goal? In the instance of being on time for work, a likely first step might be to determine if the client has a reliable way to wake up. Other steps might be, for example, to determine if the client is going to bed at a time that allows enough sleep before going to work, and finding out whether the client has reliable transportation to work.
- Next, it is important to decide on specific interventions. How will the steps be accomplished? How will the client be on time for work? Set two alarm clocks? Have a friend call to wake him or her up? Determine the closest bus stop? Not drink on workdays? Collaborate with the supervisor at work to provide verbal recognition and reinforcement of when the client is on time?
- Next, collaboratively brainstorm possible obstacles to the treatment steps and interventions. For the client who is moderating or eliminating his or her consumption of alcohol, will this mean giving up a social group? If so, how will he or she meet social needs? Will family and friends be supportive? Involved in treatment? Which ones will be supportive? What should be done about those who cannot be supportive? See them only for very short periods when alcohol is not present? These can be included as action steps and relapse prevention in the treatment plan.
- Lastly, it is very important to decide how you and the client will determine if the treatment plan is working. Will you determine this at every session? What criteria will you use? Make sure the criteria are specific and identify how you will measure them. This will allow you and the client to determine if you're on your way to Chicago or if you've made a detour somewhere!

Mary

Mary is a 53-year-old woman working as a secretary. She is divorced and cares for two of her grandchildren. She has been drinking since she was 14 and is a heavy drinker now (more than 3 drinks at a sitting and more than 9 drinks per week). Your genogram shows that there is a strong history of heavy alcohol use in her family, and that the family tends to serve alcohol at any family social occasion. Mary tells you that she wants to quit using alcohol altogether. She also wants to quit smoking. What kind of treatment plan would you put together? What would you consider? How long would you envision that Mary would need to be in treatment? What kind of social support would she need? Do you think she's depressed? Will she need referrals to a psychologist or psychiatrist? Given her family responsibilities, how frequently will she be able to be in treatment? Go to meetings?

Family, Friends, and Concerned Others in the Treatment Planning Process

Screeners and assessment batteries can provide extremely useful information about a client's alcohol use, patterns, risk of relapse, ability to cope, and motivation to change, but they don't tell you the impact on the client's family and friends or the complete story of the client's relationship with alcohol. Interviewing those closest to the client who have knowledge of the problems created by alcohol use can be very important.

This should never be done without the written permission of the client. Even if it is not required by state, province, agency, or care organization regulations, it is still important to have the client's written permission. In the United States, release of information for clients undergoing treatment for alcohol and/or other substance use disorders is mandated by a law called "Federal Law 42CFR, Part 2." Its parameters can be found on U.S. government Web pages, one of which is http://www.access.gpo.gov/nara/cfr/waisidx_02/42cfr2_02.html.

Formal written permission is commonly called a "release of information." The document, which is always kept with the client's file and a copy of which should be given to the client, allows the treating clinician permission to speak with and receive information from a designated person (or other agency). Release of information forms include specific information about the client (name, address, telephone numbers, birth date, Social Security number or other identifying number), the specific information to be released or obtained, the rights of the client to revoke the permission, and how long the release is in effect. Most also include statements prohibiting the receiving clinician or agency from turning around and releasing information to others without the client's written permission.

At times, it may be difficult to obtain the client's permission to speak with family members, friends, or other agencies or care organizations. This problem can be avoided or significantly reduced if you have a good therapeutic alliance. In talking with the client about having family involved, it is important to let clients know that the data collection is meant to help them and that their views, concerns, and opinions will be a major part of the process. One helpful analogy to relate when talking about this issue with a client goes like this: "If you were taken to the emergency room because you had chest pain, would you want one of your family members to tell the personnel there if you'd had chest pain before? If anything helped? What had happened during this bout of chest pain?"

It also can be helpful for the client to know that research into the usefulness of family involvement in the treatment of individuals with alcohol use disorders, especially in the assessment phase, can help motivate, guide, and support the client. Researchers JoEllen Patterson, Lee Williams, Claudia Grauf-Grounds, and Larry Chamow writing in *Essential Skills in Family Therapy, From the First Interview to Termination* suggest that it is also important to let clients know that there are benefits to family involvement, including "improvement in family members' satisfaction with marital and family relationships." There is a caveat, however, and that is whether family members are active drinkers with alcohol use problems of their own. Many clinicians will discourage the involvement of these family members in the assessment and treatment planning process because of the significant danger of incorrect information leading to inappropriate treatment plans.

Self Harm and Harm to Others: Initial and Ongoing Assessment

It cannot be underscored more heavily: It is critical in any intake and assessment process to determine whether clients are a danger to themselves or others. This topic was addressed in more detail in the previous chapter, but it bears repeating. You must *always* ask about the possibility of self harm and harm to others. "When people come into our agency with these kinds of problems, we always ask if they are currently thinking about or have thought about harming themselves. Have you ever attempted suicide? Given it serious thought? When was that? How did you prevent yourself from harm?" The latter question assesses the client's strengths, which can be used to help them stay safe and in treatment planning. Tell the client that this will be assessed at every appointment. Collaboratively develop warning signs of self harm with the client and ask him or her to become his or her own monitor. This helps engender self efficacy. If the client cannot guarantee safety, you must decide whether to have the client hospitalized either voluntarily or involuntarily. *Always* consult with other clinicians or administrators in your agency or care organization. If you are a physician or clinician in solo practice, consult with one or more of the professionals who you have listed in your network (see Chapter 3). If possible, help the client make this decision on his or her own. It is preferable to use a collaborative approach in this circumstance, but you have to make it clear that, if safety is an imminent issue, you must protect the client even if he or she does not want your protection.

State and provincial laws differ widely on what is known as "duty to warn" other individuals if your client has indicated that they intend to harm that person. Many times threats are vague. Consult the laws in your area for specifics. Always document what steps you have taken to ascertain potential harm.

Summing Up

Remember that the treatment plan is the map to your client's goals, but it should not be cast in concrete nor so flexible that neither you nor the client have any confidence in it. You and the client should regularly evaluate it to determine its effectiveness, and this will involve on-going assessment of symptoms. Depending upon the assessment batteries you have chosen, you and your client will want to assess symptoms, risks, and relapse issues somewhere in the middle of treatment to determine how things are going. You can do this more often. Share the results with the client and then collaboratively determine if the results are correlating well with the treatment plan.

Key Terms

ASAM. The American Society of Addiction Medicine (www.asam.org).
Assessment batteries. Two or more tests (batteries) that help a clinician determine the nature and severity of a problem (the assessment).
Genogram. A diagram of family relationships, strengths, and weaknesses. A genogram usually depicts three generations, but may be more.
Psychoactive substances. Any substance that has the ability to affect a person's mood, behavior, or thinking.

Recommended Reading

The Addictions Treatment Planner, 3rd Edition, by Arthur Jongsma and Robert R. Perkinson (Hoboken, NJ: Wiley, 2005).
Genograms: Assessment and Intervention, 2nd Edition, by Monica McGoldrick, Randy Gerson, and Sylvia Shellenberger (New York: W. W. Norton, 1999).

TRUTH OR FICTION

QUIZ ANSWERS

1. False   2. False   3. False   4. True   5. False

Treatment Tools, Programs, and Theories: Helping Clients Overcome Problem Drinking

After reading this chapter, you will be able to
answer true or false to the following statements:

1. Diving right in and starting the change process at the very beginning is the key to successful treatment. True or False?
2. There is really only one way of treating alcohol problems that has shown success. True or False?
3. Inpatient treatment is almost always more effective than outpatient. True or False?
4. There are a variety of support groups in the United States, although Alcoholics Anonymous is the most widely available. True or False?
5. There are no medications available specifically to help clients overcome drinking problems. True or False?

Answers on p. 96.

So, you've identified a client whose drinking is creating problems, and you've assessed the nature and extent of the problems. Now what? In this chapter, we will discuss various approaches to helping clients who wish to overcome problems associated with drinking.

Let's begin by discussing some of the tools that are available to help clients who have been unable to resolve their problems with drinking on their own.

THINGS TO REMEMBER

1. Although there are a variety of approaches available, the evidence is clear that no single approach works with every client. This is especially true with clients for whom personal change goals conflict with the beliefs and tenets of the treatment approach.

2. Not all alcohol-related problems require formal treatment for the client to resolve them. In fact, we know that most alcohol problems are resolved with no formal intervention or treatment at all. It is important to recognize this fact, and to not dismiss out of hand a client's commitment to a non-formal change plan.

3. Much of what happens in treatment is often counter to the basic tenets of the underlying theory upon which the approach claims to be based. This is especially true in many treatment programs that profess to adhere to a 12-step philosophy derived from Alcoholics Anonymous.

4. Treatment programs may present themselves as using one or more treatment approaches other than the 12-step approach, but in fact what they are doing is not actually those approaches. We know from survey findings that many experienced alcohol treatment clinicians who agreed that relapse prevention was a critical component of treatment of alcohol problems failed to identify the key elements of relapse prevention as also being important. The bottom line is that simply because a program professes to use, for example, cognitive-behavioral treatments does not mean that the treatments they are delivering and calling cognitive behavioral actually are.

5. As with other areas of the alcohol treatment field, there are many myths based on uncontrolled clinical anecdotes that, when explored in well-designed research, turn out to be untrue. Yet, these myths often guide how clinicians approach their clients. It is important to be aware of these myths and to understand how they may sometimes get in the way of effective change.

6. A corollary of this is that treatment programs often present what they do as being "effective" yet can offer little or no data to support the claim. In order to get the best treatment for a client, it is important that therapists ask the question: "How successful is your program, and how do you know?"

Change Tools: What's Available to Help People Overcome Drinking Problems and How Effective are Various Approaches?

Let's address the last question first. How effective are the various approaches we will discuss? The answer depends, at least in part, on what one's beliefs are about how alcohol problems are best resolved, and on the degree to which the client is ready for the interventions that the clinician has available. If continuous, prolonged abstinence from alcohol is considered the touchstone for treatment outcomes, then research findings present quite a different picture than if the touchstone is a reduction or elimination of problems associated with drinking, regardless of whether the client continues to use alcohol at some level.

Most clinicians have tended to see abstinence as most important, but it has become clear from research over the years that abstinence may not be the most important outcome indicator from the perspective of the client. While much of the research on various treatment approaches includes some measure of abstinence as an outcome, complete and total lifelong abstinence is not the desired outcome for many clients. Most alcohol problems are resolved by significant reductions in drinking and not by complete and total lifelong abstinence.

> "The expectations of life depend upon diligence; the mechanic that would perfect his work must first sharpen his tools."
>
> —CONFUCIUS

Readiness for Change as the Therapeutic "Wild Card"

Regardless of how we view the most desirable outcomes of treatment, there is another critical component to successful change: client readiness to engage in the change process coupled with client readiness to use treatment as the way to implement change. Regardless of the change methods available, whether or not the client is ready to change will determine, in part, how successful change efforts are. Readiness to change is essentially a "wild card" in the game of behavior change. While not necessarily a component of change, itself, readiness forms the basis upon which change does or does not occur.

Since the mid-1970s, researchers in addictions and health behavior change have been exploring how and why people change behavior, and conducting research that has lead to an increased understanding of the process by which change occurs. The primary focus of this research has been the Stages of Change Model (SCM, also known as the Transtheoretical Model of Change) developed by James Prochaska, Carlo DiClemente and their colleagues (Prochaska, DiClemente, & Norcross, 1993). The SCM has become a major guiding force in helping clinicians determine what treatments to introduce to clients and whether or not to focus on change at all. As a clinical heuristic, the SCM has gained wide support. Support and utilization of the SCM is so broad that it is important for us to discuss it in some detail as part of this chapter on change options. In fact, as we discuss in the next section, the idea of matching interventions to stage of change using the SCM is a cornerstone of the process of tailoring treatment to client needs. While it is important to match treatments to client attitudes and beliefs about alcohol problems, it is also important to make the focus of interventions to client readiness. How is this done?

The SCM postulates that anyone making behavior changes moves through a series of cognitive, behavioral, and emotional stages in a fixed sequence (although not at a fixed pace). These stages are detailed in Table 5.1. The stages reflect a client's readiness as indicated by problem recognition (the Precontemplation and Contemplation stages), searching for solutions once a behavior is determined by the client to be in need of change (the Preparation Stage, sometimes called Determination), and solution implementation (the Action Stage). Once solutions have been implemented, the client then focuses on maintaining the changes made (the Maintenance Stage). Sometimes maintenance efforts are successful and the behavior change becomes more or less permanent, but often the client is unable to maintain the behavior change and slips back into the previous behavior patterns (the Relapse Stage).

The various stages consist of differing cognitive, emotional, and behavioral tasks that the person goes through when making changes. In the Precontemplation stage, the behavior that may become the ultimate target of change efforts is not seen by the client as problematic or in need of change at all (Precontemplators are often labeled as being "in denial." Other people see how destructive or harmful their behavior is, but they don't). Precontemplators have been called "happy users" of alcohol or other drugs. They see no need to change that behavior.

Table 5.1: The Stages of Change Model.

Stage	Characteristics
Precontemplation	Drinking not seen as a problem, even though others may. "Happy Drinker." Ends with increased ambivalence.
Contemplation	Beginning to consider possibility that drinking is a problem. Beginning ambivalence about drinking. Ends with ambivalence resolved—moves to Preparation/Determination if in favor of changing. Recycles back to Precontemplation if not in favor of changing.
Preparation/Determination	Has decided to change but not sure how to do so. Searching for and evaluating change options. Decides on course of action and moves to next stage. May recycle back to earlier stage if unable to decide.
Action	Implementing change plans. Moves to Maintenance once change is achieved.
Maintenance	Sustaining and improving upon the change are key tasks.
Relapse	If maintenance efforts are unsuccessful, a problem drinker may relapse and, depending on the drinker's reaction, recycle as far back as Contemplation.

For many Precontemplators, however, things happen that create a focus on the possibly problematic nature of their behavior. Thus, a person who drinks alcohol may be arrested for driving while intoxicated or begin missing days of work because he or she was hungover from heavy drinking the night before. Through a process of consciousness-raising and information provision about the pros and cons of the behavior they are engaging in, many Precontemplators move into the next stage of change, Contemplation.

Contemplators have recognized that their drinking (to stick with the main example of this book!) is creating problems. Nonetheless, they may still see some advantages to continuing to drink. In the Contemplation stage, clients informally go through a cognitive evaluation process that has been formalized for use in treatment as the Decisional Balance Exercise. In this process, the client weighs the pros and cons of continuing the behavior versus changing. The pros and cons are based on the client's own view of the advantages and disadvantages of remaining unchanged versus changing. The Decision Balance Exercise form is presented in Figure 5.1.

Only when the decisional balance has tipped in favor of change (that is change is seen as personally more advantageous than continuing as before) will the person then move into the next stage of change, variously called Preparation or Determination. In the Preparation stage, the decision to change has been made ("I think I should cut down or stop drinking."), but the question of exactly how to pursue this change is unresolved. Answering that question is the focus of the Preparation stage. Again, the person casts around for options. Should I change on my own? Should I go to AA? Should I go to a treatment program? Should I try hypnosis? As in the Contemplation stage, the person weighs the subjective pros and cons of each behavior change option of which they are aware and, once one (or more) change method appears viable, makes the decision to implement a change. It is not uncommon for clients to exit the change process at this point when the change methods of which they are aware appear to be unacceptable or when the change goals that may be required by particular methods are unacceptable (e.g., the client wants to reduce drinking, but the treatment program insists on abstinence).

	Pros	Cons
Change	4	2
Don't Change	1	3

Figure 5.1: Decisional Balance Exercise sample.

Numbers refer to order in which cells are completed.

Once a change method has been chosen, the next stage, called the Action stage, involves implementing the change process using a variety of methods and strategies that have been identified by the client (often with help from concerned significant others or a clinician). Once these change methods have been implemented and initial change has occurred, the focus then shifts to maintenance of change and prevention of relapse to the old behavior.

> "Things alter for the worse spontaneously, if they be not altered for the better designedly."
>
> —FRANCIS BACON

Once the person either has solidified changes or has relapsed, the change process may either terminate with respect to that particular behavior (e.g., the behavior has been successfully changed or the client has relapsed and stopped the change process, at least temporarily), or recycle through the stages once again as the client renews and revises his or her change efforts.

It is also important to note that a client may be in a different stage of change with respect to some components of behavior than others. For example, a person may be willing to abstain from drinking alcohol in bars and be in the action stage with respect to changing the behavior of going to bars but not see drinking at home alone as problematic and, therefore, may not be ready (or in SCM terms a "precontemplator") to change the behavior of having drinks at home.

The most important implication for clinicians of the SCM is found in research done by Prochaska and his colleagues that indicates an increased likelihood of failure to change when interventions are "mismatched" to the client's current stage of change with respect to the behavior in question. Thus, attempting to engage a problem drinker who is a Precontemplator to actively change simply will not work. For clients who are Precontemplators, the focus of clinician assistance needs to be on facilitating the process of personal problem recognition and consciousness-raising with respect to the pros and cons of drinking. Telling a Precontemplator that the best way to overcome a drinking problem is to attend weekly counseling sessions and go to AA is likely to elicit a response like, "Hey, wait a minute, who says I want to stop drinking at all? I like drinking!" If the response is not that direct, putting the client in such a change program will likely result in failure that may be seen as "resistance" and "denial" when in fact it simply reflects the clinician's insensitivity to the client's stage of change.

For this reason, it is critical that clinicians assess the client's readiness to change drinking behavior at the very start of your discussions. A quick assessment can be done using a set of "Readiness Rulers" developed by Stephen Rollnick and his colleagues. The Readiness Rulers assess three components of motivation to change: Importance of Change, Readiness to Change Now, and Client Self-Efficacy with respect to changing (how confident the client is that change efforts will be successful). To use the Readiness Rulers (see Figure 5.2), the clinician first opens discussion about drinking and then asks, "How important is it for you to change your drinking right now?" Ask the client to rate himself on a scale from 0–10 with 0 indicating that the client sees no importance in changing at all, and 10 indicating that changing is the most important thing to the client right now. If importance is high (8–10) then move on to Readiness to Change Now. If readiness is high, then assess Confidence. When all three are high, the client is likely in the Preparation or Action stage of change.

Importance of Change: "How important is it for you to change your drinking now?" Please rate yourself on a scale of 0 to 10 with 0 being "not important at all to me to change my drinking" and 10 being "extremely important to me to change my drinking."

When the client rates Importance or Readiness low, the clinician can facilitate movement by asking questions such as, "What would have to happen for you to move from the rating of 4 you put on the importance of changing your drinking to, say, a 7 or 8?" Helping the client reach a conclusion that is based on his or her own sense of the value and viability of change is critical to this process. More information about how to work with the Readiness Rulers and use this process to assist clients in becoming ready to change can be found in Rollnick, Mason, and Butler's highly practical book *Health Behavior Change: A Guide for Practitioners* (1999).

What's the Best Approach?

A landmark report by the Institute of Medicine called *Broadening the Base of Treatment for Alcohol Problems* (1990) made it clear that when research findings were reviewed carefully there was no superior approach to helping people resolve alcohol problems. Nonetheless, there was a sense among the report's authors from reviewing the research literature, that if clinicians could only have available a set of rules for matching clients to specific treatments that had been shown effective for clients who shared specific characteristics, treatment outcomes overall could be enhanced.

The bottom line: About 70% of clients who are without significant co-occurring psychopathology maintain continuous abstinence in the year following completion of a course of treatment for problems with drinking. When significant co-occurring psychopathology is present, the success rate for the first year after completing treatment drops to about 50%.

0	5	10
Not at all		Extremely

Figure 5.2: Readiness Ruler: Example of importance.

The National Institute on Alcohol Abuse and Alcoholism (NIAAA) conducted a major research study aimed at identifying so-called matching variables and delineating how those variables might be used to make client-specific treatment recommendations. Project M.A.T.C.H. (an acronym for Matching Alcoholism Treatment to Client Heterogeneity) compared three manualized treatment approaches: 12-step Facilitation (TSF), which was similar to the approach used in the vast majority of alcohol treatment centers in the United States; Cognitive-Behavioral Treatment (CBT), which represented the treatment approach with the most solid research backing its effectiveness—even though it was used in very few treatment centers in the United States; and Motivational Enhancement Treatment (MET), based on motivational interviewing, which had shown great promise in helping clients make the decision to change. TSF and CBT were both 12-session treatments, while MET took only 4 sessions spread out over 12 weeks to deliver. (All three manuals are available from NIAAA at www.niaaa.nih.gov/publications/match.htm.)

Treatments were delivered by highly trained and well-supervised clinicians who were monitored to ensure that the specific treatment approach was correctly done. Clients were randomly assigned to receive one of the three treatments, but were extensively assessed on characteristics that were presumed to be important to improved treatment outcomes by proponents of the three approaches studied.

Despite the strong hopes of the researchers, few treatment-specific client-matching variables seemed to predict better outcomes with one of the treatments versus the others. All three treatments appeared to be equally effective, although the specific outcomes of the three treatments differed from one another. Thus, there were higher rates of AA attendance among clients who got the TSF treatment, which aimed specifically at helping clients understand and link to AA. Although symptoms declined equally, clients in the non-TSF treatments had lower rates of continuous abstinence. The strongest matching variable identified was a somewhat better outcome for MET among clients who were initially high on measures of anger and resistance. MET also seemed to work better for clients who were ambivalent about changing their drinking (e.g., were "Precontemplators").

To the extent that clients affiliate with support groups after treatment, these outcomes seem to be improved. It is not yet clear, due mainly to lack of research, whether the specific nature and content of the support group is important or not. Only AA is very widely available to those desiring support to resolve drinking problems, although alternatives are growing both in number and in membership. There is also increasing use of online support groups, although the effectiveness of online support has not been adequately tested. Even with support groups, the question of the nature of the desired outcome is important. For clients who do not want prolonged abstinence, successfully pursuing a program of moderate drinking may be the desired outcome. At least one support group, Moderation Management (MM), supports people in pursuing non-abstinence goals.

Despite the focus of Project M.A.T.C.H. on three approaches, there are a number of other approaches to helping people with alcohol problems that have garnered significant research support. The Community Reinforcement Approach (CRA) and its companion program for concerned significant others (CSOs), Community Reinforcement and Family Training (CRAFT) have been shown over and over to be a useful way of helping clients become engaged in changing problematic drinking and in remaining engaged in that process. There is also some evidence supporting the effectiveness of several medications with some clients. Disulfiram (Antabuse®), naltrexone (ReVia®) and acamprosate (Campral®) all have have been found to help some clients resolve drinking problems.

Treatment approaches can also be more prolonged or briefer in duration. There is substantial research supporting the use of relatively brief interventions for people with alcohol problems. Recall that one of the successful treatments in Project M.A.T.C.H., was MET, a shorter four-session treatment. Nonetheless, for many other clients, more prolonged treatment and support may be both desired and necessary. To the extent that the clinician can work collaboratively with the client, and often with the client's family members, in designing an intervention process that the client is willing to commit to strongly, the more likely it is that a positive outcome will result.

So what's available to help clients achieve a positive outcome, assuming that the client is either unwilling to pursue a self-change intervention or has been unsuccessful at self-change? We will briefly outline several formal approaches to working with alcohol problems that either have wide professional acceptance or that have substantial research supporting their effectiveness. The formal approaches we will consider are Twelve-Step Based Treatment (TS), Cognitive-Behavioral Treatment (CBT), Motivational Interviewing (MI), CRA/CRAFT, brief interventions (BI), and medications. These are not mutually exclusive approaches. There is evidence, for example, that one or two sessions of MI prior to entering either a TS or CBT treatment can enhance the effectiveness of those treatments. Likewise, BI tend to have components that overlap significantly with MI, as do both CRA and CRAFT. There is even an approach to working with medications called the BRENDA approach (Volpicelli et al., 2001) that combines all of these approaches!

In helping clients decide on a formal intervention, it is extremely helpful for the clinician to have some familiarity with these options, as well as knowledge of which programs in the client's local region provide these options. While space permits only a brief recounting of the theory and practice of each approach, readers who are interested in more extensive discussions might consider reading

Treating Substance Abuse: Theory and Technique, 2nd Edition edited by F. Rotgers, J. Morgenstern, and S. Walters.

Twelve-Step Approaches

Chances are that if a client wants a formal treatment program, some aspect of 12-step philosophy will be a part of it. In fact, a survey several years ago by the National Institute on Drug Abuse found that more than 90% of treatment programs that responded used 12-step philosophy or some aspect of it as a component of their treatments. Ironically, it is only in the past decade or so that research supporting the effectiveness of these approaches has been developed. In contrast to other treatments for medical conditions ("diseases") in the alcohol problems field, 12 steps became the most widely used treatment with little solid evidence supporting its effectiveness. Nonetheless, for clients who strongly commit to following the tenets of the 12 steps and who do so as a part of a formal treatment program and self-help support group following treatment, there is good evidence of success in maintaining prolonged abstinence from alcohol.

TS treatment grew out of a "professionalization" of the 12-step philosophy of Alcoholics Anonymous (AA). AA was developed in the mid-1930s by two alcoholic men, Bill Wilson and Dr. Bob Smith. It grew from two small groups to a worldwide organization that now claims several million members and tens of thousands of groups. The 12 steps represent a spiritually based program of recovery that also contains a number of behavioral steps that the client is encouraged to pursue as part of an overall lifestyle change. The 12 steps are presented in Table 5.2.

Treatment based on the 12 steps has several components. The first of these is a strong emphasis on introducing the client to the 12 steps and to 12-step meetings. The formal treatment approach most often used is one based on the 12-Step Facilitation (TSF) approach developed by Joseph Nowinski, which formed the basis for one of the treatments in Project M.A.T.C.H. TSF focuses on educating that client about the 12 steps of AA, helping overcome doubts and resistance to various aspects of the AA philosophy (for example, many clients initially have difficulty with the notion of a "higher power"), and introducing the client to a variety of behaviors that are considered to be supportive of prolonged (if not lifelong) abstinence from alcohol. These include accepting that one is an "alcoholic" and can only get into "recovery" by abstinence from alcohol, attending AA meetings, developing a relationship with a sponsor, abstaining from alcohol and other abusable drugs, avoiding high-risk situations, reaching out to other AA members when one is tempted to drink, changing one's lifestyle ("people, places and things") and working through the 12 steps of AA in the context of regular meeting attendance and reading of AA literature.

TSF and derivative TS approaches place a heavy emphasis on teaching the client helpful slogans ("one day at a time," "first things first," "easy does it") that serve as cues and reminders to the client about how to live a life of recovery. While the

Table 5.2: The 12 Steps of Alcoholics Anonymous.

1. We admitted we were powerless over alcohol—that our lives had become unmanageable.

2. Came to believe that a Power greater than ourselves could restore us to sanity.

3. Made a decision to turn our will and our lives over to the care of God as we understood Him.

4. Made a searching and fearless moral inventory of ourselves.

5. Admitted to God, to ourselves and to another human being the exact nature of our wrongs.

6. Were entirely ready to have God remove all these defects of character.

7. Humbly asked Him to remove our shortcomings.

8. Made a list of all persons we had harmed, and became willing to make amends to them all.

9. Made direct amends to such people wherever possible, except when to do so would injure them or others.

10. Continued to take personal inventory and when we were wrong promptly admitted it.

11. Sought through prayer and meditation to improve our conscious contact with God, as we understood Him, praying only for knowledge of His will for us and the power to carry that out.

12. Having had a spiritual awakening as the result of these steps, we tried to carry this message to alcoholics, and to practice these principles in all our affairs.

original literature of AA suggests that people can recover from alcohol problems, TSF and TS approaches present the process of recovery as one of lifelong duration and required vigilance lest the abstinent client find himself or herself on a slippery slope back to problematic drinking. TSF and TS approaches view alcoholism and alcohol problems as resulting from a disease that is spiritual, genetic, and biological. It is a disease that can never be cured, but can be kept in remission. For this reason, it is a basic tenet of TSF and TS approaches that a lifelong affiliation with AA is critical to achieving and maintaining abstinence from alcohol.

For TSF and TS approaches, the only successful outcome of treatment (and resolution of alcohol problems without treatment, for that matter) is lifelong abstinence from alcohol (and often other non-prescribed psychoactive substances, as well, although cigarettes seem to have largely escaped this prohibition of psychoactive substances) achieved "one day at a time." Given research on actual treatment outcomes, this is often a difficult goal for most clients to reach. For this reason, TSF and TS approaches present alcoholism as being a "chronic, relapsing disease." This means that the client is always at risk of returning to problematic drinking, unless attention to recovery and recovery-promoting activities is maintained.

Failure of the client to maintain abstinence is often viewed as a sign of denial, which must be penetrated and broken down in order for abstinence to be successfully maintained. This often involves confronting clients with the errors in their thinking (from the TS clinician's perspective) and attempting to help them shift their thinking more toward the need for maintaining abstinence as the basis for recovery. Failure to maintain abstinence is also frequently attributed to the workings of the disease, as well as failure to "work the program" (e.g., attend meetings, meet regularly with one's sponsor, etc.). When clients have difficulty maintaining abstinence, the solution usually proposed by TS therapists is for them to intensify their involvement in AA. In fact, one slogan often heard in AA meetings, but one that is not a part of AA itself, is "90 meetings in 90 days," indicating that the best way to effectively recover is, in effect, total immersion in AA and recovery activities immediately following formal treatment.

Given the ubiquity of TSF and TS approaches, helping clients who find aspects of them objectionable presents a major challenge to clinicians who choose not to be the ones who treat their clients' alcohol problems. There have been, until very recently, few other options for clients who prefer to attempt moderation rather than a treatment goal of lifelong abstinence. Thus, despite the recognition by the developers of AA that non-abstinent resolutions of alcohol problems do occur (see pp. 31–33 in *Alcoholics Anonymous*) and substantial research suggesting that such outcomes are the rule rather than the exception, it is a basic requirement of TSF and TS approaches that abstinence be the goal adopted by the client. This may be one reason why many clients resist TS approaches initially. They have not yet reached the stage of change in which they have decided that abstinence is the best course for them. From the TS perspective, such clients are considered to be in denial and need to be worked with to recognize the supposed danger associated with a non-abstinent drinking goal. Often this process seems to belittle or contradict client beliefs and can be perceived by clients as being quite negative (even though well intentioned on the part of TS clinicians). For the clinician working to assist a client overcome problem drinking, this is an important aspect of TS approaches to be aware of, and it's something the clinician should be prepared to discuss with the client. It also behooves the clinician to be aware of other, less abstinence-focused alternative treatments that will be discussed next.

Cognitive-behavioral Treatments (CBT)

CBT developed out of behavioral learning theories and studies of both animal and human behavior dating back to the early 20th century. In contrast to TS approaches, CBT views alcohol problems as resulting from learned behavior and not from a spiritual, genetic, and biological disease. According to CBT, problematic alcohol use is maintained by a combination of classical conditioning (e.g., association of environmental or internal cues with the experience of intoxication), operant conditioning (e.g., association of the behavior of drinking with the reinforcer of pleasant feelings), modeling (e.g., seeing others behave in particular ways as a result of alcohol consumption), and cognitive processes including expectancies regarding the effects of alcohol (e.g., "if I drink I'll be sexier," "more relaxed," etc.) and cognitive distortions related to drinking (e.g., "I need a drink" or "I can't function socially without being high").

The specific change methods used in CBT derive directly from these processes. The focus in CBT is on helping clients develop and implement skills that will enable them to avoid problems associated with drinking. Thus, the person who craves alcohol during social situations in which he or she feels anxious and has a belief that alcohol is "needed" in order to effectively interact with members of the opposite sex, would be taught how to relax in social situations without alcohol, as well as social interaction and conversational skills to facilitate interactions without drinking.

Goal-setting in CBT is done collaboratively with the client, not unilaterally by the treatment provider as is the case in virtually all TS programs. The touchstones of treatment outcome are achievement of individualized goals that are derived from a thorough behavioral analysis of the client's drinking and the factors associated with it. Using a method called "functional analysis" in which the client and therapist collaboratively identify antecedent stimuli/behaviors/feelings to drinking, the actual behavior that occurs in response to these antecedents, and the specific consequences (reinforcers) that ensue, the therapist and client develop an intervention plan aimed at interrupting the change of antecedents, behaviors, and consequences and, thus, disrupting or preventing drinking.

A heavy emphasis is placed in CBT on the development of a strong therapeutic alliance with the client that is based on a collaborative, respectful, and empathetic stance by the therapist. In the context of this alliance, the keys to helping clients whose goal is abstinence are to identify high-risk situations (those that assessment has revealed are ones in which the client has been highly likely to drink to excess in the past), avoid them if possible (e.g., helping the client develop an alternate route home from work that does not pass by the client's favorite cocktail lounge!), or learn coping responses if avoidance is not possible (e.g., teaching the client how to say "no" to an offer of a drink).

For clients whose goal is reduced use, rather than abstinence, helping the client identify the factors and situations associated with overdrinking and develop strategies for preventing overdrinking form the critical tasks of therapy. Given that moderate drinking is based on empirically derived drinking guidelines (e.g., no more than 4 standard drinks per occasion for males, with no more than 4 drinking occasions per week, and for females no more than 3 standard drinks on no more than 4 drinking occasions per week), developing techniques for keeping track of how much one has consumed, avoiding consumption in situations in which overdrinking is likely (e.g., when emotionally upset, if the client has tended to drink heavily under those circumstances in the past), and developing behaviors that facilitate slower drinking of less alcohol (e.g., sipping rather than taking large swallows, spacing drinks over time, etc.) are all part of helping clients reduce drinking to safe levels.

Ongoing and repeated assessment is critical to success in CBT. Unlike TS approaches, CBT places heavy emphasis on the therapist as an evaluator and strategy developer. In contrast to TS approaches, where failure to achieve treatment goals is attributed to factors presumed to be internal to the client (e.g., "denial" or "not working the program"), failures to achieve client goals in CBT are viewed, at least partly, as a failure by the therapist to adequately assess the client's drinking and teach effective coping and change strategies.

CBT places a premium on tailoring treatment activities to specific client needs. Thus, assessment becomes much more critical than it is in TS approaches where a nearly uniform approach is taken toward all clients (e.g., attend meetings, call your sponsor, avoid people, places, and things associated with drinking, etc.).

Working with client thinking is important in CBT, just as it is in TS approaches. However, the CBT approach relies on techniques developed by schools of cognitive therapy to help the client recognize, through experiential "experiments" and gentle challenges of the client's thinking ("what's the evidence that alcohol makes you more attractive to members of the opposite sex?"), rather than on direct confrontation or labeling of client thoughts as being indicative of "denial."

CBT approaches are, by their nature, time limited. Because CBT views alcohol problems as being learned rather than as a result of factors inherent in the client (e.g., a biologically predisposed disease), permanent change is viewed as an achievable goal. Thus, while CBT practitioners will often suggest that clients attend support groups (there are now two support groups that are based on CBT principles), sometimes even AA, the role of the support groups is viewed differently than is the case with TS approaches. Support groups in CBT are seen as places in which the client can interact with and model the behavior of others who have been successful at resolving alcohol-related problems. They are also seen as places where the client can practice new behaviors and thinking with the ultimate view toward making the changed behaviors and thoughts permanent. At some point, for many clients, behavior change is presumed to have solidified to the extent that no further treatment or support is necessary. While clients may not be able to "unlearn" or "forget" conditioned responses associated with alcohol use, they can learn new, reliable alternative thoughts and coping behaviors that need not be continuously reinforced over a lifetime.

One of the cornerstones of CBT is its emphasis on Relapse Prevention (RP). RP was originally developed within a CBT framework by clinical psychologists G. Alan Marlatt and Judith Gordon (Marlatt & Gordon, 1985) and later taken up and adapted to a TS perspective by addictions counselor Terrance Gorski.

RP relies heavily on identifying high-risk situations for drinking, developing strategies for coping with those situations without drinking, and developing strategies for coping with failures to cope (e.g., drinking when one had resolved to be abstinent or drinking more than moderate limits). Marlatt and Gordon identify the source of many relapses to what they called the "abstinence violation effect" or AVE. For those with non-abstinence goals, this has also been called the "limit violation effect." The AVE consists of a series of personal attributions that the client makes about the meaning of taking a drink once abstinence (or reduced drinking) has been asserted as his or her drinking goal. In relapses (as opposed to lapses or slips in which drinking occurs, but the client does not return to pre-change levels of consumption), research has shown that clients often attribute their drinking to stable, internal factors ("I'm a bad person," "I'm an alcoholic and there's nothing I can do about it") and essentially cease efforts at managing drinking behavior. Clients often develop catastrophic negative thoughts about themselves when slips happen, particularly if their peers, family and others are heavily invested in supporting lifelong abstinence. The negative emotions that result often further exacerbate the slip into a full-blown relapse. Helping the client to restructure this thinking ("I only drank in that one situation," "Having a drink doesn't make me a failure; it simply means I had a drink," "I can resume abstinence again") is an important part of keeping slips or lapses from becoming full-blown relapse.

Finally, CBT is heavily invested in measuring outcomes, both for individuals and for groups of clients. While TS approaches have become increasingly invested in scientific measurement of outcomes, this approach has been a cornerstone of CBT since its inception. Thus, hand in hand with ongoing assessment is measurement of outcomes, not only in terms of drinking parameters (quantity/frequency) but other associated indicators of improvement such as maintaining employment, fulfilling one's obligations to family and work, and improved physical health.

Motivational Interviewing (MI)

MI represents a decided departure from both TS and CBT, at least as the latter was originally conceptualized. While TS and CBT both place a heavy emphasis on therapist expertise in helping clients overcome alcohol problems, MI focuses on developing and enhancing the client's own strengths as a means of promoting changes in drinking behavior. MI was developed initially by psychologist William R. Miller of the University of New Mexico in collaboration with Stephen Rollnick, a psychologist in Wales. Miller had been working in a setting where he encountered many addicted clients, but, contrary to the experiences reported by his addiction counselor colleagues, he seemed to encounter no denial of drinking problems among his clients. In fact, his clients would often tell him in great detail about their substance use and the negative consequences that resulted. This lack of denial issues among his clients piqued Miller's interest, and he began investigating the possibility that it was the therapist who created denial rather than denial being a characteristic of clients with alcohol problems.

Following an extensive review of the research literature on motivation and on interpersonal communication, Miller proposed a research-based explanation of denial. According to Miller, denial was a normal human process that typically occurred when a particular type of communication pattern was established between two people, one of whom was engaging in a behavior about which he or she was ambivalent, meaning the behavior was viewed as both beneficial and positive, but also carried some negative consequences with it. The communication pattern involved Person A (the therapist) telling Person B (the drinker for whom drinking had both positive and negative aspects) that drinking was a problem and should be changed. In fact, Person A took the "drinking is bad" side of Person B's ambivalence. When this happens in dyadic communication studies, Person B almost always argues the other side of the ambivalence ("Hey, drinking isn't so bad. I enjoy it."). From the perspective of Person A, though, this signals a denial of the downside of alcohol use! The way out of this dilemma is for the therapist to stop arguing that drinking is bad and instead to focus on the client's ambivalence about drinking. This process constitutes the core of MI.

This process of helping the client focus on and resolve ambivalence about drinking is accomplished through a particular set of therapist behaviors that Miller and Rollnick have summarized in the acronym OARS. The therapist asks Open-ended questions, Affirms the client's struggling with ambivalence, Reflects client statements, particularly highlighting ambivalence, and Summarizes client statements and views, with particular attention to repeating "change talk," which are those indications that the client is considering change. During this process, the therapist maintains an empathetic stance and attempts to understand the client's views from the client's perspective. Nonetheless, the therapist also has expertise to offer. And once the client begins to show signs of resolving ambivalence toward change (what Miller and Rollnick call "change talk"), the therapist reinforces this resolution by explicitly reflecting those client verbalizations that point toward change (e.g., "I'll think about it," "Maybe I need to do something," "I really need to stop drinking").

Miller and Rollnick (2002) have explicated a variety of strategies and tactics that clinicians can employ in helping clients move toward change talk. Some of these are listed in Table 5.3. Most require some practice in order for the therapist to implement them effectively. However, even simple reflections are useful in accomplishing the main goals of MI: to make the client feel heard, supported and understood, while helping the client resolve ambivalence in a way that will be productive. This emphasis on the client being at the center of the change process and directing it from his or her own perspective is underscored by Miller and Rollnick, who caution against using MI when the therapist has a specific change agenda (e.g., drinking goal) in mind. MI is most useful when the client arrives at a resolution that is of his or her own choosing. The more a client's

Table 5.3. Sample Tactics of Motivational Interviewing.

1. Simple reflection: mirroring what the client has said with little change.
2. Double-sided reflection: "on the one hand . . . on the other hand . . . "
3. Amplified reflection: mirroring with exaggeration.
4. Shifting focus: shifting attention away from perceived stumbling blocks.
5. Reframing: acknowledging validity of the client's view, then offering a new interpretation of the underlying facts.
6. Agreeing with a twist: reflection followed by a reframe.
7. Emphasizing personal choice and control: reinforcing that the client is always in charge of his or her behavior.
8. Coming alongside: defending the counterchange side of the argument.

Source: Miller and Rollnick (2002).

change efforts are characterized by a sense of personal autonomy and choice, the greater the likelihood that the client will stick with change efforts, even in the face of difficulties. MI aims to enhance this sense of personal autonomy in clients.

Once the client begins to make a commitment to change his or her drinking (regardless of whether the extent of the initial proposed change comports with the therapist's idea of how and to what extent the client "should" change) the client can be considered to be moving toward the Preparation stage of change. Here, again, the MI process becomes useful in helping the client choose among a variety of possible change options. In fact, early on in their writings about MI, Miller and Rollnick identified six components of an effective motivational intervention (these components also characterize effective brief interventions for alcohol problems) that they summarized in the acronym FRAMES (see Table 5.4). An important component of FRAMES, but one often omitted by treatment providers in their approach to clients, is the provision of a Menu of change options from which the client might choose in directing his or her change efforts.

Once the client has moved from Precontemplation/Contemplation ("I don't have a problem with drinking." to "Maybe I should do something about my drinking.") to Preparation ("I wonder what I should do about my drinking, and how I should go about it?") the MI process begins anew. At this point, the degree to which the therapist is conversant with different options and treatments available, the more likely it is that the therapist will be able to help the client choose a change process to which the client can strongly commit. Using the same techniques of OARS coupled with Decisional Balance Exercises, the therapist can help the client decide on a course of action and build commitment to sustaining it.

Table 5.4: FRAMES.

• Clinician provides non-judgmental, respectful Feedback to client.
• Responsibility for change is acknowledged to rest squarely with the client.
• Nonetheless, the clinician may give specific Advice as to how or what to change.
• A Menu of options for change is provided and discussed with the client.
• Empathy characterizes the clinician's interaction style.
• Clinician Supports self-efficacy, instilling hope that change is possible.

Source: Miller and Rollnick (1991).

Once a course of action is decided, the therapist again shifts roles and becomes an "expert" on how other people have been able to make lasting behavior changes. Now the therapist is a teaching resource for the client who needs training or other guidance in the implementation of an effective change plan. Once a set of change options has been chosen, the therapist may suggest a variety of approaches to change, including options that are part of both TS and CBT approaches to treatment. However, the therapist does not prescribe these approaches unless the client requests a prescription. Rather, the MI process is used to assist the client in making his or her own decisions about how to proceed. The therapist then provides resources in the service of this effort, which the client is also free to accept and use or reject.

MI is highly compatible with both TS and CBT change approaches. It helps the client "set the stage" for change, and make a commitment to pursuing the change process actively.

Inpatient vs. Outpatient: Which is Best?

As with virtually every other question we have asked in this book, the answer to this one is "it depends." First off, we should point out that, contrary to public perception, there is no evidence that inpatient treatment programs are more effective than outpatient programs. In fact, nowadays, with the advent of managed care, it is unusual for a client to be able to secure third-party reimbursement for more than a few days of inpatient treatment. The "28-Day Rehab," as portrayed in such movies as"28 Days" is largely a thing of the past, except for clients who have top-of-the-line insurance or who can afford to pay for treatment themselves.

That being said, there are some instances in which at least a brief inpatient stay may be warranted and should be suggested to the client as an option. Inpatient treatment seems to be most strongly indicated in cases where the client has a history of withdrawal symptoms and is currently drinking very heavily (in which case a medically supervised detoxification may be needed if the patient is to initiate abstinence), in cases where the client has few external resources supportive of change or is living a disorganized or chaotic lifestyle (e.g., is homeless, unemployed, or has no family), or in cases where the client is suffering from other medical or psychological disorders that may require more intensive observation and treatment around the clock (e.g., client has pancreatitis or has become suicidal while intoxicated). In these latter instances, the clinician may have some legal or ethical responsibility to supervene a client's personal wishes and use coercive means to get a client into a facility against the client's expressed wishes (e.g., the client is acutely intoxicated and unable to hold a discussion about options, or the client is homicidal or suicidal and needs to be civilly committed for his or her own protection or for public safety). In all other cases, however, these options should be discussed with the client, and the pros and cons assessed for that client at that time. Clinicians should become familiar with the laws where they practice with regard to involuntary hospitalization should this become necessary to prevent a client from harming self or others.

In most cases, effective treatment can be provided with no inpatient stay. Most alcohol detoxification can be accomplished on an ambulatory basis with medical oversight and prescription of supportive medications, such as Librium. Behavioral treatment can also be effectively accomplished on an outpatient basis, even for clients who meet criteria for alcohol dependence.

There are three general forms of outpatient treatment available for patients whose drinking goal is abstinence: outpatient, intensive outpatient, and partial hospitalization. For clients whose goal is to reduce drinking but not to stop altogether, there are often clinicians in the community (as well as an increasing number of treatment programs) who will provide moderation-focused treatment if the client is unable to make changes on his/her own. The clinician or client will need to ask local programs and alcohol treatment providers whether or not nonabstinence goals are supported by the agency or treating clinician. For clients whose goal is abstinence, however, many more resources are available, and most programs will support that goal.

The main difference among the three forms of outpatient treatment is in the number of treatment sessions per week and the number of hours the client will be asked to spend at the treatment provider's site. Outpatient treatment programs typically meet for 1–3 hours per week either in individual or group therapy formats. Intensive outpatient programs extend programming to two or more days per week, typically 4–6 hours per day. Finally, partial hospitalization programs typically ask that the client be on site daily or nearly daily for the entire day, only leaving the site to go home to sleep.

The decision of which outpatient treatment to use can be made using the ASAM Patient Placement Criteria outlined in Chapter 4. However, as noted there, these criteria have stood up well to research into their relationship to treatment outcome. Another decision-making rule a clinician might apply is the "stepped care" rule developed by Linda and Mark Sobell. The "stepped care" rule suggests that the least intensive, least restrictive treatment option that has not already been tried by the client be the first choice for intervention (unless there are clear reasons to opt for a more intensive or restrictive approach, such as medical problems or a need for supervised detox). Once that treatment has been tried, it should be evaluated and, if the client has been successful in achieving his or her treatment goals, it should be terminated. If the client has failed to achieve his or her treatment goals in a less intensive/restrictive setting, then the clinician and client should discuss the possibility of implementing a more intensive level of treatment.

The "stepped care" process has the advantages that it conserves both client and treatment program resources, ensuring that only clients who need more intensive treatments get them as the first choice. A fair analogy would be that we don't start treating a minor headache with brain surgery because that operation should be reserved for those whose headaches are due to brain tumors! It also allows for a gradual intensification of treatment to levels that the client has not had previously, thus increasing the likelihood of success. A third advantage is that clients can build upon earlier experiences with less intensive programs to improve the likelihood of success with a more intensive option later. Finally, "stepped care" makes more sense for clients who are unwilling to commit strongly to either the goals or intensity of more intensive treatment programs because it gives the client and clinician previous experiences that form the rationale for a higher level of care. This ensures that a client is involved and strongly committed to whatever treatment intensity is chosen, rather than imposed on the basis of criteria that may seem arbitrary to the client.

Medication

The use of medication to assist problem drinkers resolve their drinking problems has been quite controversial. Believers in a drastic, completely drug-free life have often vocally advised problem drinkers to avoid even essential psychiatric medications. This has been known to happen in some AA groups, and prompted the General Service Office of AA to publish a pamphlet on the "The AA Member-Medication and Other Drugs" urging AA members to work closely with and comply with medically prescribed medications to treat diagnosed conditions, even psychiatric ones.

Medications serve two purposes in the treatment of alcohol problems. For more severely dependent drinkers, medications are an important part of most detoxification procedures. The goal of medically managed detox is to make the process more comfortable for the client (thus increasing the likelihood that the client will detox completely) and to control or altogether avoid the risk of grand mal seizures which are the main life-threatening possibility when heavy drinkers stop drinking suddenly.

The usual detox procedure involves substituting a sedative/hypnotic medication with a longer metabolic half-life for alcohol, which is a short acting, short half-life sedative/hypnotic. The usual practice is to put the client on Librium, a benzodiazepine, and vitamin supplements. Heavy alcohol consumption can interfere with absorption of nutrients from food, particularly B vitamins, and vitamin therapy reverses that and forestalls possible alcohol-related dementia. The dose of Librium is then gradually tapered over several days to prevent seizures and keep the client comfortable during withdrawal.

The second major use of medication to help people resolve alcohol problems is as a direct adjunct to behavioral treatment. There are currently three medications approved by the FDA for treatment of alcohol problems: disulfiram (marketed as Antabuse®), naltrexone (marketed as ReVia®) and acamprosate (marketed as Campral®). Each medication has different uses and interactions.

Disulfiram was the first medication approved specifically for treatment of alcoholism and is most widely known. It works by inhibiting the enzyme in the stomach that eliminates acetaldehyde, one of the toxic byproducts of alcohol metabolism, from the body. When a client taking disulfiram drinks even a small amount of alcohol he/she immediately begins to have a buildup of acetaldehyde in the body with accompanying headache, nausea, increased blood pressure, and malaise. There are precautions against using any product that might contain alcohol while taking disulfiram because in some clients ingestion of even a small amount may trigger the drug reaction. Some clients describe the disulfiram reaction as being like an extremely bad hangover. The assumption in prescribing disulfiram is that knowing the discomfort that will come from ingesting alcohol prevents the client from drinking. For many clients, this does appear to happen. However, disulfiram must be taken daily (one treatment approach mentioned earlier—Community Reinforcement—includes monitored administration of disulfiram as part of its protocol), and not all clients actually experience the disulfiram reaction. In fact, some clients discover through testing that they are able to drink despite being on disulfiram. Nonetheless, for motivated clients and, perhaps most importantly, binge drinkers who are trying to avoid the next binge, disulfiram can be a useful adjunct to behavioral treatments.

Naltrexone and acamprosate both have a similar effect, but they operate through somewhat different biological mechanisms. Both seem to reduce the intensity of the subjective experience of alcohol consumption, thereby reducing the rewarding effect of drinking, and they also seem to dampen the desire to drink to some degree. Both drugs have been shown to be effective adjuncts to help motivated problem drinkers remain abstinent when they're administered in the context of a behavioral treatment program. Naltrexone also has been studied as an adjunct to behavioral self-control training for clients whose drinking goal is moderation. The research on this use of naltrexone is quite promising, but its use for this purpose has not yet been widely accepted.

All of these medications require some caution in their use, particularly with patients whose drinking has resulted in liver or other gastrointestinal problems. In addition, naltrexone cannot be used by anyone taking opiates because it blocks the analgesic effect of the opiates on the brain receptors. However, research has shown them to be useful adjuncts to behavioral treatment for patients who are motivated to use them.

The Role of Support Groups in Helping Clients Overcome Alcohol Problems

In the United States, use of support groups has formed the core of traditional treatment for alcohol problems. In fact, a recent study of self-help groups for alcohol and drug problems commissioned by the Veterans Affairs Administration reported the following findings with regard to self-help groups:

(1) They are the most frequently accessed resource for alcohol and other drug problems, (2) Over six million adults a year have contact with addiction self-help groups, (3) Organizations based on the "twelve steps" (e.g., Alcoholics Anonymous) are larger and more available than non-12-step organizations, (4) Important alternatives to traditional drug and alcohol self-help groups exist both for individuals desiring a different approach, and, for individuals experiencing a comorbid serious psychiatric disorder. (Workgroup on Substance Abuse Self-Help Organizations, 2003)

There are many support groups available both in face-to-face and online formats that provide assistance to their members in both reaching their treatment goals and lifestyle changes and in maintaining the changes the member has made. The value of support groups (particularly AA for people who self-identify as "alcoholics") is well documented by research, and they have the unique advantage of being generally free of charge, requiring no financial resources in order to access help. Nonetheless, it is critically important that clinicians recognize that support groups are not universally effective or helpful. As with any other change method we have discussed, the use of support groups by a particular client needs to be tailored to a variety of factors. These factors should be discussed openly and non-judgmentally with every client as part of the process of defining a problem resolution strategy that the client can make a commitment to. In the remainder of this chapter we outline some of these factors.

Self-Selection and Choice

First and foremost, self-help groups are exactly that, "self" help groups. For this reason, they work best for those who choose to affiliate with them. In fact, this has been explicitly recognized on an anecdotal level as long ago at the founding of AA and the writing of The Big Book when Bill W. outlined AA's program of

Selected List of Self-help Support Groups

Alcoholics Anonymous (AA)	Most widely available with groups world-wide and more than 2 million members. Abstinence and spiritual focus. Website: www.alcoholics-anonymous.org
Self Management and Recovery Training (SMART)	Cognitive behavioral model of alcohol problems. Abstinence focus with both face-to-face and Internet support. Website: www.smartrecovery.org
Women for Sobriety (WFS)	For women only. Focus on empowerment message. Abstinence focus. Face-to-face and pen pal programs. Website: www.womenforsobriety.org
Secular Organizations for Sobriety-Save Ourselves (SOS)	Non-spiritual alternative to AA. Both face-to-face and Internet support. Website: www.secularsobriety.org
Moderation Management (MM)	Only group to support both abstinence and reduced drinking goals. Cognitive behavioral orientation. Both face-to-face and Internet support via email and chat rooms. Website: www.moderation.org

attraction. This sort of finding is a virtual truism. Nonetheless, traditional treatment programs and providers have had a tendency to prescribe rather than suggest self-help group attendance to clients. When clients, following this prescription, have found the particular suggested group not to their liking, the clinician's or program's response often has been to blame the client for being resistant or in denial, rather than questioning the prescription. Until recently, there were virtually no alternatives to AA available anywhere. Now, however, as shown above, a number of alternatives have arisen, largely in response to client unhappiness with one or more aspects of AA. There are now a variety of options from which clients, particularly those living in larger urban regions, can choose. There are even self-help groups that provide support largely via the Internet.

Drinking Goal

With the exception of Moderation Management™ (MM), all self-help groups available in the United States focus on the goal of complete, lifelong abstinence from alcohol. If a client is interested in, for example, abstaining for a period of time and then reconsidering that decision in the future, that person will often find it difficult to discuss this interest openly in an abstinence-focused group, even one that is non-12 step. For clients who are ambivalent about lifelong absti-nence, a suggestion that they explore MM may be most appropriate. MM sup-ports both abstinence (for a period determined by the client) and moderation goals, as well as making lifestyle changes to enable a healthier life generally.

Belief or Disbelief in Disease Model Accounts of Alcohol Problems

Over the years AA has developed, at least in some meetings, a version of the dis-ease model of alcohol problems that suggests that if one is "alcoholic" (e.g., has self-defined as such) then one has a disease which precludes any drinking at all, ever. While the founders of AA were agnostic about defining alcoholism as a dis-ease, the adoption of AA philosophy by the alcohol treatment industry as the dominant theory of practice has led to more and more people entering AA both from treatment programs (as opposed to being self-referred) and the criminal justice system. These people have often been taught a version of the disease model as a way of both explaining their alcohol problems and reinforcing the need for continued vigilance lest relapse occur.

For people seeking help with alcohol problems who have not been through traditional treatment or who don't buy into the disease model of alcohol prob-lems, it can be an exercise in frustration and a primary cause of resistance in treat-ment for a practitioner to insist that the client attend AA. For such clients, suggesting that they explore some of the non-disease model alternatives such as SMART Recovery, Women for Sobriety, or Secular Organization for Sobriety may allow the client to obtain free support without evoking resistance to disease or other 12- step concepts (such as its spirituality) that some clients may find objectionable.

Comorbid Psychopathology

While self-help group attendance is very useful for many clients, for some it can be a nightmare. For example, a client who suffers from social phobia may find the very act of sitting in a roomful of people highly disturbing. Clients who are prone to become dependent upon others may also be poor candidates for self-help groups that can become a dominant (but not always helpful) focus of the client's life. As with other aspects of helping clients change alcohol use, a thor-ough assessment of the client can be instructive to the clinician in helping the client to decide whether or when to attend self-help groups.

Availability

Of all the support groups listed in the Useful Resources box, AA is by far the most available. In fact, it has been said that, particularly in larger urban areas there is always an AA meeting happening. In rural areas, even AA may be less available, however, and the effort required simply to get to a meeting may make self-help group attendance onerous. Some support groups (including AA) are now developing a strong Internet presence in the form of email lists and support chat rooms. However, this process is still in its infancy. One support group, MM, provides the vast majority of its support online through email or chat rooms. Given MM's openness to both abstinence and non-abstinence goals, and its non-spiritual nature, it may be a useful option for many clients. For clients who have many obligations in their lives (work, family, school) availability of self-help options may become a major factor in determining which to use. Given that, on average, clients prefer easier rather than more difficult approaches to resolving problems, helping clients find available support that fits into their lives is an important task with which the clinician can help.

Summing Up

As we have seen, there are many formal ways clinicians can help clients resolve problems with alcohol. The clinician's challenge is helping clients define which of these many options is right for them. Given that none of these options is demonstrably superior to the others, and that all have research supporting their effectiveness with some clients, our view is that the clinician's role should be exploring the options with the client, trying to elicit the client's commitment to an initial course of action, and supporting his or her follow through. Once the client has followed through with a change plan, the clinician and client can then evaluate the success of the plan and plan for discharge and relapse prevention.

Key Terms

Readiness to change. Concept developed by Prochaska and colleagues as the Transtheoretical Model of Change that refers to a client's readiness to consider and make changes in drinking behavior. It is important to assess readiness, as a mismatch between clinician actions and client readiness will likely lead to treatment drop-out or failure.

Commitment. Regardless of the pathway to change selected by the client, the degree to which the client has a strong commitment (signified by intentions and actions) to pursue that pathway is an important predictor of treatment success.

Motivational Interviewing. Approach developed by William Miller and Stephen Rollnick that uses a directive, client-centered process of relating to clients to help them work through ambivalence about change and make a commitment to a course of action.

Cognitive-behavioral therapy. Approach to helping clients change that is rooted in behavioral psychology. Has strong evidence for its effectiveness.

Twelve-Step Facilitation. Manualized approach to helping clients who have chosen abstinence as their drinking goal to understand and affiliate with 12-step support groups such as Alcoholics Anonymous.

Support groups. Frequently helpful aspect of change efforts by clients that provide support for changes within a nonprofessional context. Best when clients choose the group with which they wish to affiliate.

Recommended Reading

Addiction and Change: How Addictions Develop and Addicted People Recover, by C. C. DiClemente (New York: Guilford, 2003).

Handbook of Alcoholism Treatment Approaches: Effective Alternatives, 3rd Edition, edited by R. K. Hester and W. R. Miller (Boston: Allyn & Bacon, 2003).

Treating Substance Abuse: Theory and Technique, 2nd Edition, by F. Rotgers, J. Morgenstern, and S. T. Walters (New York: Guilford, 2003).

TRUTH OR FICTION

QUIZ ANSWERS

1. False   2. False   3. False   4. True   5. False

CHAPTER 6

When and How Should Clients Be Discharged to Aftercare?

TRUTH OR FICTION

QUIZ

After reading this chapter, you will be able to answer true or false to the following statements:

1. Aftercare is only necessary if a client has been at an inpatient treatment center. True or False?

2. There are several types of aftercare that can be considered. True or False?

3. The therapist is the only person who should determine what kind of aftercare is necessary. True or False?

4. There is no such thing as recovery for the client who has an alcohol problem. True or False?

5. Recovery is a long-term process that requires a variety of types of support. True or False?

Answers on p. 107.

What Is Aftercare?

Suppose you were in the hospital following surgery. Your surgery went well. Your stitches are healing. You've been up and walking, and you've been allowed to eat solid food again. One day, the nurse comes in and says, "You did GREAT! Pack your bags. You're out of here! Good luck!" What would you do? You might panic. Certainly you would be confused and worried. You might think: I haven't a clue what I'm supposed to do now. Do I need to take medication? Am I supposed to have physical therapy? Can I go back to work? When am I supposed to see the doctor again? What if I have pain? What if I have other symptoms? What if my problem comes back?

All licensed hospitals have personnel who help patients do something called discharge planning. This is a plan for making sure that the gains made by the patient in the hospital continue after he or she leaves the hospital. It is usually very specific and contains everything from what medicines to take to arrangements for

> "Finishing races is important, but racing is more important."
>
> —DALE EARNHARDT

therapy to handling contingencies for possible relapses. The plan usually calls for continued contact with the professionals who treated the problem or who will take over from those who did. It may call for extended at-home care or a stay in a rehabilitation facility, if needed. It will specify if medications are needed and how they will be taken. It will specify if the patient needs certain equipment such as a walker, wheelchair, cane, crutch, or sling. It may require follow-up therapy at home or at a specialized locale. In the field of alcohol use disorder treatment, discharge planning is usually called "aftercare," although the two terms are often used interchangeably in both fields.

Aftercare planning for the treatment of alcohol use disorders can be simple or complex. In "28 Days," the comedy-drama about substance use rehabilitation, persons leaving rehab were reminded on their way out, "Remember 90 meetings in 90 days and ask for help." That can be construed as aftercare, but it shouldn't be. Aftercare planning needs to be do-able, organized, detailed, and specific. Remember how important specificity was in treatment planning? For the same reasons, aftercare should be specific as well. A specific plan makes it easier for the client and for you to track ongoing recovery, to plan for or avoid problems, and to recognize individual issues before or as they arise. And, as we've said before, the ingredients in any aftercare planning must be achievable.

In Cognitive Behavior Therapy (the empirically validated type of therapy that teaches patients about how their thoughts affect their feelings and their behavior), patients are given regular "homework" assignments to accomplish in between sessions. Homework has been shown to shorten the time a patient is in therapy and make it more effective, but it's not successful if the patient can't or won't do it. Aftercare, like homework, has to be achievable.

But before we get started on the how's, why's, and wherefore's of aftercare, let's take a look at what has to happen first: deciding about discharge.

How Do You Know If the Client Should be Discharged to Aftercare?

Remission—and, later, recovery—can be defined in a number of ways. Some of the definitions stem from the model of treatment that has been used. Other definitions come from the *Diagnostic and Statistical Manual of Mental Disorders, Fourth Edition*. Researchers John Finney, Rudolf Moos, and Christine Timko, writing in *Addictions, A Comprehensive Guidebook*, define remission as "abstinence, non-problem drinking, or substantially improved drinking." Long-term remission—usually 5 to 10 years—is often construed as recovery, though this is open to debate. Long-term remission rates are encouraging. In 12 studies conducted from 1982–1993, 21% to 83% of individuals studied who survived achieved long-term recovery.

Formal Terms from the *DSM-IV*

As you learned in Chapter 1, one of the most commonly used methods of diagnosing substance use (including alcohol) disorders is the *Diagnostic and Statistical Manual of Mental Disorders, Fourth Edition, Text Revision (DSM-IV-TR;* American Psychiatric Association, 2000). It details the cognitive, behavioral, and physiological symptoms or criteria that describe substance use disorders. The criteria for remission are defined by the amount of time that criteria—or partial criteria—have been met or not met. It also describes the definitions associated with full and partial recovery. The terms are:

- *Early Full Remission*—This term is used for individuals who haven't met any of the criteria for Dependence or Abuse for at least one month, but less than 12 months.
- *Early Partial Remission*—This term is used for individuals who no longer meet one or more of the criteria for Dependence or Abuse for more than 1 month, but less than 12 months.
- *Sustained Full Remission*—This term is used for individuals who haven't met any of the criteria for Dependence or Abuse at any time during a period of 12 months or more.
- *Sustained Partial Remission*—This term is applied to individuals who do not meet the full criteria for Dependence or Abuse for 12 or more months, but one or more criteria have been met.

There are two other descriptors that must be mentioned: On Agonist Therapy, and In a Controlled Environment. These descriptors portray a client who may be on, for example, benzodiazepine treatment to prevent seizures during withdrawal from alcohol (agonist therapy), and second, one who has been in a rehabilitation situation where access to alcohol has been restricted (in a controlled environment). The client who now requires aftercare planning may or may not be in a controlled environment. It is unlikely that an individual will be on agonist therapy during aftercare, but they may be receiving other medications such as acamprosate (Campral)—which is known as an antagonist because it is thought to reduce the pleasurable effects of alcohol ingestion—or medication for other problems such as depression. This, of course, requires the supervision of medical personnel and must be specified in aftercare planning.

Most clients emerging from an intensive period of treatment, perhaps including inpatient rehab, will be in Early Full Remission or Early Partial Remission. Typically, they have had some success reducing or eliminating their intake of alcohol for at least one month and no more than 12 months. Depending upon the aftercare program, continued remission and eventual discharge will be ascertained by self-report, by therapist evaluation, and by testing.

DSM-IV criteria are not the only aspects of recovery you and your client will be considering. As you have read, people attempting to make changes of any kind in their lives go through stages of change. The same is true of remission and recovery. Recovery is not a destination as much as it is a process. Each stage of change reflects the motivational level of the client. The most widely used model of change was created by James Prochaska, John Norcross, and Carlo DiClemente. It is known as the "Transtheoretical Model" because it isn't tied to a particular theory of change or recovery and has been used widely in alcohol and other treatment. It is commonly known as the "Stages of Change Model."

While other theorists have proposed expansions to the model, the original model consists of five stages:

- **Precontemplation.** This is the stage where clients do not recognize that there is a problem, or if they do recognize a problem they believe it to be someone else's problem, not theirs. Individuals who are court-ordered to treatment are almost always in the precontemplation stage.
- **Contemplation.** In this stage, clients do recognize that there is a problem, are thinking about how it might be managed, but are unsure about how to deal with it or whether it can actually be dealt with. It is during this stage and the next stage that you are first likely to see the client who is voluntarily interested in treatment. They have many questions and require a very supportive therapeutic relationship.
- **Preparation.** During this stage, clients actively collect information about how to cope with the problem and solicit help. They often think about troubleshooting problems related to their alcohol use disorder: "If I go to rehab, will I still have a job when I get out?" "It's embarrassing to admit I have a problem. How will I tell my family?" "How much is this going to cost me? Will my insurance cover it?" "Can I really do this?"
- **Action.** The name of this stage is self-explanatory. The client puts into action the plan for dealing with problem drinking and monitors progress. It is during this stage that clients often have a great deal of drive, but can find themselves in risky situations that set them up for relapse because they have not completely identified the pitfalls in their individual recovery. They also are beginning to understand what role alcohol played in their relationships, their work, and their recreation. The early commitment to recovery—sometimes called the "pink cloud" because everything in the sober life seems optimistic and achievable— is at risk during the action stage because changes are not yet permanent and unexpected problems can arise.
- **Maintenance.** During this stage, clients have made and maintained over time the changes necessary to eliminating problem drinking. It is during this stage that therapists will want to review successes and detail the reasons that the successes were achievable. In early maintenance, clients may have a great number of fears about relapse. They may have achieved remission before and then reverted to old routines and drinking habits.

See if you can determine which stage of change the following clients are in:

1. Harry suspects he may have a problem with alcohol use. He has seen some evidence that there is a problem. For example, he just got his first driving under the influence (DUI) citation, and his doctor is concerned that Harry's abdominal pain may be due to his drinking. Harry isn't sure what he can do about this situation, but he's begun looking at the books in the Addictions section of his local bookstore to see what he can find out. (Answer: Contemplation)

2. George has just been released from prison where he served 18 months for breaking and entering. As part of his probation, he has been court-ordered to treatment for alcohol use problems. George gets angry thinking about this because he considers himself a "weekend warrior," drinking a couple of cases only on weekends, not someone who has a drinking problem. (Answer: Precontemplation)

3. Florence has been abstinent from alcohol for more than a year. Everyone who knows her congratulates her on her achievement, but Florence is still not completely assured that she will not relapse. So, she schedules periodic "booster sessions" with her therapist just to make sure she stays on track. (Answer: Early Maintenance)

In the original Stages of Change model, time frames were included for each stage. For example, it was suggested that a client was in the contemplation stage if he or she intended to take action within about six months. Later research suggests that people can remain in the contemplation stage for many years before moving into preparation. Other research suggests that people move fluidly back and forth between stages before permanent maintenance is achieved.

During aftercare, you may want to assess how the client is doing by the use of functional assessment instruments. There are a variety to choose from. See Chapter 1 for suggestions.

If they have never achieved maintenance before, they may be unable to envision what it really will look like. For clients who have achieved long-term remission, aftercare may consist of occasional meetings with a therapist ("booster sessions"), group participation, or even involvement in helping others.

Types of Aftercare

Taken at its simplest, aftercare suggests stepped-down treatment following a period of more frequent and more intense treatment for alcohol use problems. This permits a great deal of flexibility in designing aftercare therapy, but the purpose is clear: The gains made in the more intense treatment need to be maintained, and planned aftercare is designed to make that more possible than no aftercare.

There are several types of aftercare. Which type is dependent upon the goals the client has set for himself or herself, the type of original care, insurance coverage, the client's legal status, and the client's work and family situation.

> "In completing one discovery we never fail to get an imperfect knowledge of others of which we could have no idea before, so that we cannot solve one doubt without creating several new ones."
>
> —JOSEPH PRIESTLY

Halfway Houses

Halfway houses, also known as recovery homes, sober living accommodations, or transitional living, are commonly recommended for the client who is coming out of inpatient rehabilitation or who is under court jurisdiction. Some alcohol treatment centers with inpatient facilities also offer halfway house treatment, usually in the vicinity of the main facility. The client lives in the halfway house but is likely to return regularly to the inpatient facility for group and individual therapeutic work. A halfway house program offers the client a place to stay and, usually, a rigorous program requiring the client to work, to have set curfews, and to participate formally in house activities such as group and individual therapy and informally in house maintenance and socializing with other house residents. House rules may also require that clients participate in 12-step or other community-based programs of care. Halfway house treatment is usually 6 to 12 months in length but can vary considerably.

Partial Hospitalization or Intensive Outpatient Treatment

Rarely, but occasionally, clients who have been in inpatient treatment are referred for aftercare to partial hospitalization programs or intensive outpatient treatment. The former is less common than it used to be because of cost, but programs still exist. Partial hospitalization is a very intensive day or day-into-evening program where clients live at home, but attend group and individual treatment sessions usually up to eight hours a day.

Intensive outpatient treatment, despite its name, is less intensive in time than partial hospitalization. Clients involved in this treatment usually attend group therapy and didactic sessions four hours a day. For those who are working, the sessions are usually held in the evenings, but many programs offer day and evening sessions to accommodate clients' schedules.

Depending upon insurance, these types of aftercare can last one to three months. Individual and group counseling continues sometimes for up to a year, usually on a weekly basis. Almost all partial hospitalization or intensive out-patient aftercare treatment plans call for the client to submit to random urine or breath testing, and attend regular 12-step or other support groups along with group and individual counseling. Clients who are under legal jurisdiction during this time will also have their attendance and test results reported to the court. Test refusal, failing a test, or spotty attendance is likely to mean jail time.

Outpatient Aftercare

In outpatient aftercare, the client attends at least one therapy session per week and is often required to attend a set number of 12-step or other support groups per week as well. Random urine or breath testing is conducted during this period. Treatment consists of continuing the support the client needs to main-tain treatment gains, as well as to set future goals both for alcohol use problems and for "life" problems such as education, work, and relationship issues. Most clients are "stepped down" to outpatient aftercare from partial hospitalization, intensive outpatient treatment, and inpatient treatment. It is the most common form of aftercare. This type of aftercare usually lasts three to six months, but it can last longer with decreasing frequency if the client is doing well.

Discharge from Aftercare

Discharge from aftercare is usually determined by a therapist. Some of the crite-ria for discharge include an extended period of testing clean, regular attendance at group and individual counseling sessions, regular attendance at 12-step or other community-based groups that may include finding a sponsor, compliance with court requirements, holding a steady job, and self-assessment of progress. Just as treatment planning is a collaborative effort between therapist and client, so, too, is discharge planning.

Treatment involves looking at the whole person, not just his or her alcohol use problems. For example, if you went to your doctor and found out that you were suffering from diabetes, you can be sure your doctor would not just hand you a prescription for medication. The doctor would talk with you about your diet or refer you to a dietician who could help you with that part of your life.

Aftercare for the Client with Dual Diagnosis

You will recall from previous chapters that alcohol use disorders commonly co-occur with depression, anxiety, and other serious health problems. If you and your dually diagnosed client are now planning aftercare, on-going treatment for these other problems has to be included. During treatment, the client may have learned about self-monitoring. This is a technique where clients identify their particular symptoms and rate them on a simple severity scale, say zero to five. A zero would represent no symptomatology, and a five would represent serious

Discharge Planning

- How much "clean time" has there been?
- Have there been any lapses or relapses? How many? How long? How severe? What did the client learn from the lapses or relapses?
- Is the client holding a steady job?
- Does the client regularly attend individual therapy sessions? Family therapy sessions, if referred?
- Is the client taking care of himself or herself in other ways, such as taking prescribed medications, eating right, getting exercise, getting enough sleep, developing appropriate and healthy pastimes?
- How are the client's relationships? With whom is he or she socializing and are they supportive of the client's recovery?
- How does the client spend his or her leisure time?
- How is the client managing money?

symptomatology perhaps requiring hospitalization. For example, for the client who suffers from depression, individual symptoms might be sleep disturbance, lack of appetite, feeling depressed, having trouble concentrating, and being fatigued. The client would place a number on the self-monitoring chart for each of these symptoms to rate that day's severity. The client might also track how compliant he or she has been in taking prescribed medication. Each day, the client rates the presence and severity of symptoms. The corresponding number (0–5) is usually written down on a chart designed for self-monitoring, but it can also be written down on a calendar. As part of aftercare, you and the client will agree on what number requires a phone call to you, to the professional providing medical treatment for the problem, or to the local hospital if the problem is urgent or emergent. A scale for alcohol craving or number of thoughts about alcohol during the day is also usually developed. Through this, the client may find that as the symptoms of his or her depression creep up, so do cravings. You and the client will also determine what number on the scale requires a telephone call to you or a special therapy session to reaffirm commitment to goals and plans to avoid relapse. Self-monitoring is a powerful tool because it begins to put control of the client's life back into his or her hands, and learning to stay in control of one's life is the major goal of aftercare.

Assessing Community Resources

After reading Chapter 3, you probably have a good list of professionals to whom you can refer or who provide good consultation. They should be a "first stop" on the road to assessing the resources available in your community. You will want to make a list of these resources and keep notes on both professionals' and clients' opinions of them. Some resources start out being terrific, but perhaps because of a change in management, a drying up of funding streams, a loss of key personnel, or other issues, the quality begins to slip. When this occurs, it will be important for you to assure yourself that they are still providing high-quality care or you and the client will not want to use them for aftercare until the quality improves. One way to do this is by designing a feedback form that tracks a variety of aspects of aftercare. Figure 6.1 provides a short example of a feedback form.

If part of aftercare planning includes group participation such as AA or Women for Sobriety, you will want to stay updated on availability of local meetings. The AA Website (www.aa.org) lists available meetings by community and state, but these are not always updated. You will want to contact the groups in your community to make sure that times, dates, and places are accurate.

What do you do if there are no resources in your community? First, assess whether your client would be willing to commute to a nearby community that does have resources. Ask your professional contacts to help you determine what resources are available in that community. *Remember*: the harder it is for clients to find and participate in recovery supports, the more difficulty they are likely to have in maintaining treatment gains. As we mentioned earlier in this chapter, aftercare must be feasible or it will not be successful. You may want to consider organizing recovery support yourself or in cooperation with other therapists in your community who treat clients with alcohol use disorders. You will want to discuss this with others in your organization, assess liabilities and find out legal ramifications, but this is how many recovery support groups get started.

Please read each question carefully and answer the question by circling the number that corresponds to your reply. Please do not write your name on this form.

	Not at all	Somewhat	Most of the time	All of the time
1. I am respected.	1	2	3	4
2. I have learned a lot about my alcohol problems.	1	2	3	4
3. My counselor and I work well together.	1	2	3	4
4. I would recommend this program to others.	1	2	3	4

Figure 6.1: Feedback form.

Family and Friends in the Aftercare Setting

An individual's problems with alcohol use were once considered to be the problem of the individual. About 30 years ago, that view changed when research clearly demonstrated that family members could be part of the problem and were also part of the solution. The family is now considered to be so important that the Joint Commission on the Accreditation of Health Care Organizations (JCAHCO) has a requirement for certification of substance use treatment programs that an adult family member living in the household be at least part of the assessment process.

Just as the individual usually proceeds through a series of stages in remission and recovery, so do the family and friends of the person with alcohol use problems. While there are several models of family recovery, generally families go through stages that include tension, anxiety, disbelief, tentative belief, concern about success, concern about relapse, and adjustment to a life that is not organized around alcohol. Researcher and author Stephanie Brown, writing in *The Family Recovery Guide*, suggests that, much like the individual with alcohol use problems, the family of the individual goes through four stages: the Drinking Stage, the Transition Stage, the Early Recovery Stage, and the Ongoing Recovery Stage. During the family recovery process, they must learn to "recognize that the behaviors and thoughts that seemed so extreme and dangerous were in fact understandable and grew out of a complex system that was in place."

This understanding and the progress through the stages requires therapeutic support for the family. Usually this consists of individual counseling, education about alcohol use disorders and their sequelae, learning coping skills, and having group support.

Some family members are not supportive of remission and recovery when they discover that a major effort must be made and that it may include them. Others stop being supportive when they find that the changes in their loved one, though beneficial to the family, also meant changes in lifestyle, personality, and family dynamics. Again, this requires support for the family as the individual goes through aftercare and proceeds through remission and recovery.

One issue that often arises among family members is the question of how do we know that the client is being truthful with us about being in recovery and can we do urine monitoring or use some other objective way of ensuring that our loved one is not drinking again? The typical answer to families and others who ask this question is to say, "You can never be absolutely sure, but the best way to be reasonably confident is to develop a strong channel of communication with your loved one and to be understanding as well as supportive." We also suggest educating family members about the variability in recovery from alcohol problems. By preparing them, the discovery of a loved one's relapse can be met with a productive reaction rather than a destructive one.

On the issue of biological monitoring, we generally discourage any use of it that is not requested by the client. In Appendix B, we review our own clinical rationale for using biological monitoring as an aid in recovery.

Key Terms

Aftercare. Formal or informal treatment of an individual who has been released from more intensive treatment for an alcohol use problem.

Agonist. A substance that has the ability to mimic a naturally occurring substance. For example, the generic medication benzodiazepine mimics alcohol at the cellular level. Agonists are used in treatment usually to prevent withdrawal symptoms.

DSM-IV. *The Diagnostic and Statistical Manual of Mental Disorders, 4th Edition.* A listing of mental disorders and the criteria required to be diagnosed with them.

Recovery. The process of overcoming alcohol use problems.

Remission. Long-term recovery.

Recommended Reading

The Recovery Book by Arlene and Howard Eisenberg and Al J. Mooney (New York: Workman Publishing, 1992). Though this book maintains a focus on complete sobriety as opposed to moderation, it has many useful supports for anyone trying to address alcohol use problems.

The Family Recovery Guide: A Map for Healthy Growth, by Stephanie Brown (Oakland, CA: New Harbinger Publications, 2000).

Changing for Good, by James O. Prochaska, John Norcross, and Carlo DiClemente (New York: Avon Books, 1994).

TRUTH OR FICTION

QUIZ ANSWERS

1. False   2. True   3. False   4. False   5. True

CHAPTER 7

How to Increase Recovery Success, Minimize "Slips," and Avoid Chronic Relapse

After reading this chapter, you will be able to answer true or false to the following statements:

1. If a person abstains from alcohol, one drink will "set him off" on a relapse. True or False?

2. The goal for anyone with an alcohol use disorder is to be completely substance free. True or False?

3. A clear, specific relapse prevention plan can significantly reduce the chances of having a lapse or full-blown relapse. True or False?

4. Relapse prevention requires not only addressing alcohol use but also learning how to manage thoughts and feelings about one's whole life. True or False?

5. Although early intervention in relapse is preferable, it is possible to intervene at any point in the process. True or False?

Answers on p. 124.

The Problem of the "Failure" Label

What if you were on a diet and the first time you ate an "illegal" cookie your nutritionist (or spouse or support group) pronounced you a "treatment failure?" How would you feel? Would you be eager to continue eating healthily? Would you think to yourself, "Heck, it was just one cookie. I know what went wrong and I get can back on track?" Or would you think, "What's the use? I've failed. I might as well have more cookies. I was never meant to be thin anyway?"

Unfortunately, the latter statement represents the way many clients with alcohol use disorders think and feel about lapses, relapse, and their chance of recovery. It is even more problematic that the field of alcohol use disorder treatment has not always agreed on the definition of the words. At one time, *any* posttreatment

> "Certain situations, certain friends have to be avoided to avoid a relapse."
>
> —LEIF GARRETT

use of alcohol was considered tantamount to a "treatment failure," and occasionally this is still the case. Relapse meant failure. The client who got sober and stayed sober was a "success"; the client who got sober and then had a lapse—even if alcohol use was no longer really a problem in his or her life—was considered a treatment failure. Furthermore, although the client who lapsed or relapsed was considered a "treatment failure," the field of alcohol treatment almost always considered alcohol use problems to be chronic relapsing disorders. Confusing? Yes.

Let's look at the data for some clarity. Statistics clearly show that rates of resumption of alcohol use for individuals attempting to become abstinent are high—approximately two-thirds in the first 3 months after treatment—and fewer than 35% are able to remain abstinent during the first year following treatment. Some estimates of relapse rates during the first year following treatment range close to 50% (www.treatment.org). Researchers Lori Quigley and G. Alan Marlatt write that "for a large proportion of individuals treated for addictive behavior, resumption of substance use is the most likely outcome."

This kind of data can sound depressing for both the client and the therapist! But does it mean that any posttreatment use of alcohol means "failure?" No. What it really underscores is the importance of clear, specific, organized, and proactive posttreatment recovery planning, and enhancing self-efficacy.

Lapse and Relapse

Before we talk about relapse prevention, theories, strategies for preventing problems, dealing with triggers, creating "stay safe" plans, and providing support for the recovering client, let's take a look at the definitions of two of the important terms we'll be using throughout this chapter: *lapse* and *relapse*. Organizations such as the Treatment Improvement Exchange (www.treatment.org) have defined *relapse* as "the process of becoming dysfunctional in recovery." They define *recovery* as "abstinence plus a full return to bio/psycho/social functioning." This is similar to the idea that any return to alcohol use, however brief, is a "failure." Not everyone agrees with this. Quigley and Marlatt consider a lapse to be "an initial return" to alcohol use "or a transgression of one's goal." That goal may be moderate or sporadic use of alcohol that does not cause problems in the client's life, or it may be abstinence. Relapse is then a return to pretreatment status or problematic use. Lapses don't always presage a relapse—it is a myth that one drink will always set someone off on a full-blown relapse—but lapses are clear warning signals that the client is at risk for relapse. They are also warning signals that if there is no clear, organized, and specific plan for relapse prevention, now is the time to collaboratively create one with the client.

Assessing Relapse Potential

Quigley and Marlatt state that during the very first session of relapse prevention work with a client "a detailed assessment of substance use and substance-related risk behaviors is conducted." They suggest using the following questions for assessment:

- When did initial use take place, and when was the last period of use?
- During the last period of use, what was the quantity and frequency of use?
- How long was the period of maladaptive use?
- How long was the longest period of abstinence or nonproblem use?
- What was the largest amount of alcohol used during this period?
- Are there any signs of physical dependence such as tolerance and withdrawal that may require medical supervision?
- What psychosocial stressors exist, such as job or school problems, legal problems, relationship issues?
- How is the overall health of the client?
- Are there any indications of co-occurring psychological or psychiatric problems such as depression or anxiety?

Barbara McCrady, writing in the *Clinical Handbook of Psychological Disorders, Third Edition,* emphasizes the importance of assessing previous attempts to quit: "Many clients have successfully decreased or stopped drinking on their own at some time," and this factors not only into treatment but into relapse planning as well.

There are formal instruments for assessing relapse potential (see Chapter 1), but it is also possible to use decision matrices, genograms, and autobiographies of the client to assist in this process.

What Is Relapse Prevention?

The objective of relapse prevention is to maintain the goals achieved in treatment, and to proactively address situations that have the potential to become problems for the client. These goals may be abstinence or a reduction in problematic use. Quigley and Marlatt write that "the goals of RP [relapse prevention] are twofold. The first goal is to prevent a lapse . . . so that a full-blown relapse . . . is less likely. The second goal is successful management of relapse episodes, if they do occur, to prevent exacerbation or continuation of maladaptive substance use."

In 1985, Marlatt and J. R. Gordon developed what was designed to be a maintenance program for individuals who had been in treatment. The treatment goals of these individuals were to reduce, moderate, or eliminate alcohol or substance use. The objective behind the development of the maintenance program was to augment and perpetuate treatment gains so that individuals were not constantly in a "revolving door" of treatment-relapse-treatment. The foundation of their model was the idea that individuals were not "treatment failures" and "victims of an underlying disease process," and that lapses and even relapse were not evidence of failure, but understandable parts of a recovery process in which a client was learning new ways to think, cope, and behave. As Quigley and Marlatt wrote, "Lapses . . . and relapses therefore, are part of a learning process rather than a final outcome of treatment." They pointed out that a 1996 study found that "endorsement of a disease model of alcoholism was strongly predictive of relapse by six months. This suggests that the way clients conceptualize their substance-related problems, including their attributions of controllability, may play a key role in successful behavior maintenance." In other words, abstinence may not always be the goal, and that viewing alcohol use problems within a disease model does not necessarily help clients to believe they can succeed.

Fostering Hope and Self-Efficacy

The idea that alcohol problems are not part of a disease model, but are learned thought processes and behaviors that can be unlearned, fosters hope and self-efficacy. It allows the therapist and the client to collaboratively identify the individual risks facing the client, then help him or her to brainstorm and implement healthy, appropriate ways to avoid or cope with those risks. Quigley and Marlatt wrote that "treatment utilizing the RP approach is empowering and trains individuals to act as their own therapists with regard to managing addictive behavior patterns." Much the same approach is now successfully taken with individuals who have mental illnesses separate from alcohol use problems. Becoming one's own therapist is a prominent feature of treatments such as cognitive therapy for depression, bipolar disorder, and anxiety disorders.

> "Rather than viewing a brief relapse back to inactivity as a failure, treat it as a challenge and try to get back on track as soon as possible."
>
> —JIMMY CONNORS

Relapse Prevention 101

In 1980, Marlatt and Gordon analyzed more than 300 relapse episodes. These episodes involved not just alcohol use, but other addictive behaviors as well, such as cigarette smoking, heroin use, overeating, and gambling. They identified three determinants that accounted for more than 70% of relapse situations:

1. Negative emotional states (such as anger, anxiety, frustration, boredom, depression)
2. Interpersonal conflict
3. Social pressure to use

They also found other determinants that accounted for the balance of the relapse episodes:

- being sick or injured
- feeling happy and positive

CASE STUDY

See if you can determine which of the following individuals is at risk for a relapse. Remember that a "relapse" is defined as a return to pretreatment status or problematic drinking.

1. Catherine is a 35-year-old mother of three. She has been successful in moderating her drinking for about 6 months, but lately she has been fighting with her husband, is worried about her job, and has started associating with an old friend who used to be a drinking buddy.

2. Rick is 26. He recently moved 1,200 miles away from his family to take a job in a new city. He is emotionally very close to his family and he misses them. But he has located a support group near his office, and he has been asking members to recommend a good therapist in the area. He also recently started an exercise program.

3. Jorge is 53 and recently divorced. More than 20 years ago, he became abstinent from alcohol, but since his wife left occasionally he goes to the bar after work and has a few beers with some buddies. Two weekends ago, he had a barbeque and invited some friends who decided to bring a couple kegs. Jorge acknowledges that that night he drank a lot and actually doesn't remember much about the evening.

- pushing the limits (how much control do I really have?)
- experiencing urges or temptations
- experiencing positive interpersonal feelings and situations

The determinants previously mentioned allow great specificity as well as latitude in helping clients identify and target their particular risk factors. We will talk more about this later in this chapter, but identifying these potential pitfalls allows clients, for example, to track moods, to identify and track the incidence of arguments or fights that have preceded use, and to recognize what social situations and other environments are problematic. This, then, is the foundation for relapse prevention or "stay safe" plans.

The relapse prevention model has a very distinctive view of persons who exhibit behaviors consistent with alcohol use disorders. Its basis is that (1) these behaviors are caused by multiple factors, (2) each cause must be addressed, and (3) relapse isn't a place but a process, a continuum from nonproblem use to problem use. At any point, a client may be anywhere along that continuum. Relapse prevention (and treatment) must address the place along the continuum where the client is. Also, as mentioned before, in relapse prevention, addictive behaviors are viewed as learned behaviors. Quigley and Marlatt wrote that:

*To the extent that a substance is used to cope with unpleasant situations, expe-
riences, or emotions, the behavior may also be viewed as a learned maladaptive
coping strategy. Such habits may be learned through a combination of both classical and operant conditioning processes, which may not be under the individual's direct control. Individuals struggling with addictive behaviors, therefore,
are not held accountable for the development of an addiction, just as they are
not held responsible for their learning histories.*

Any relapse prevention plan needs to address the determinants or risk factors
that seem common to relapse episodes. For example, the client who has alcohol
use problems may have inadequate social skills, poor coping skills, inaccurate
thinking, or physical, mental, or emotional problems. He or she may have completed treatment but be concerned about his or her perceived control over what
was once problematic use.

How the "Thinking" Factor Works

All of these factors have at their core how the client thinks. One modern form of
treatment for numerous problems including alcohol use disorders, cognitive
behavior therapy, evolved from the work of Aaron Beck, Albert Ellis, and Donald Meichenbaum. The fundamental postulate of this form of treatment is that
thinking affects feeling and behavior, and that influencing any one of these
aspects can influence the others. For the client with alcohol use problems,
relapse dangers can occur at any one of these sites (thinking, feeling, or behav-
ing), as can relapse prevention.

Using cognitive behavior therapy as a foundation, Marlatt and his colleagues
created a model of the relapse process. It is conceptualized as a flow chart, and
it begins with a behavior change that includes a client's sense of perceived control. At the next step on the flow chart, the client encounters a high-risk situation. In the high-risk situation, the client can make one of two choices: to utilize
a coping response or not. If the client chooses not to use a coping response, does
not have one prepared, or has not practiced the coping response prior to the
high-risk situation (very important!), the model suggests that this will lead to
decreased self-efficacy plus the belief that using alcohol will be a good thing (feel
good, increase socialization, etc.). A lapse then follows. The client understands
that this is a violation of his or her goals for recovery, and he or she may begin to
feel guilt and a perceived loss of control. This sets the stage for an increased
chance for relapse. However, if the client who has entered a high-risk situation
utilizes a predetermined and practiced coping response, he or she experiences
increased self-efficacy and perceived control, and the chances of relapse lessen.

A word about the importance of perceived control. As Davis, one of the coauthors of this book, wrote in her doctoral dissertation (2004), which examined
perceived control in a variety of domains, "The importance of perceived control
in people's lives is vast. Indeed, there is much research to support the notion that

the perception of control is as important, if not more important . . . than[,] actual control."

In 1996, Ellen Skinner emphasized and expanded on the importance of perceived control: "When people perceive that they have a high degree of control, they exert effort, try hard, initiate action, and persist in the face of failures and setbacks; they evince interest, optimism, sustained attention, problem solving, and an action orientation." Sound like something important to a client hoping to recover from alcohol use problems? Absolutely! More specifically, this means that it is critical for clients with alcohol use disorders to create, practice, and understand how to appropriately use the tools necessary to help them address high-risk situations successfully. Success then increases their sense of control and self-efficacy, and when that occurs they are less likely to experience lapses or proceed to full-blown relapse.

Enhancing Self-Efficacy: The Power of Accurate Thinking

Albert Bandura, a well-known and respected researcher in the field of socially learned behavior and self-efficacy, has defined self-efficacy as "beliefs in one's capabilities to organize and execute the courses of action required to produce given attainments." Simply put, self-efficacy is the perception that you have what it's going to take to get organized and start doing what it is you want to achieve. Where do these beliefs come from? They come from the client's own experiences, what other people say about the client's ability to accomplish goals, and the client's own thoughts about his or her ability to accomplish goals.

So how do you help the client enhance his or her self-efficacy? Despite what you may have heard about the power of "positive thinking," it's actually *accurate* thinking that is a major foundation for enhancing self-efficacy. For example, if the client who is concerned about relapse has a long history of relapses, encouraging him or her to think, "I can do this. Nothing will stop me." isn't well supported by experience. The client has had numerous relapses. The flip side of that coin is that there have also been numerous periods when his or her drinking was under control. With better planning for and awareness of the signals of impending lapses, relapse becomes significantly less likely. So their new thought is going to have to be accurate: "I have been able to moderate my drinking many times, and I now have set up ways that I can reduce the chances of lapses."

Creating accurate thinking is challenging and takes practice. You will want to work with the client consistently to examine his or her thoughts and to determine how to make them more accurate. Accurate thinking greatly enhances self-efficacy by increasing problem-solving abilities, which, in turn, further enhances self-efficacy.

Triggers: People, Places, Things, and More

There are multiple definitions of the verb *trigger*: activate, cause, generate, prompt, or set off. They all imply the beginning of something. In the case of alcohol use disorders, *trigger* means a conditioned cue or anything that starts a client on the road to lapse or relapse. Triggers are highly individual. As Marlatt and Gordon identified, they can be—and are likely to be—negative emotional states. For example, one of the coauthors of this book once saw a client who drank 8–10 ounces of alcohol only before bed. Why? Because he was an anxious person, and, for him, bedtime meant putting his head on the pillow and then being held captive by all the distressing thoughts and images from that day, that week, or even his entire life. He wanted to escape all that. He wanted to drink enough that he would be barely conscious when his head hit the pillow. One of his triggers was the feeling of anxiety. Another trigger was the accompanying thought "I can't get to sleep without alcohol." These triggers were enough to maintain his drinking behavior, which had caused physical problems for him, as well as prompting arguments between him and his wife. During treatment, he was taught how alcohol actually interferes with sleep. He was also taught to recognize the precursors of his anxiety (the approach of bedtime for his children and then for him and his wife). Finally, he was taught to practice specific relaxation techniques (diaphragmatic breathing and guided imagery) for 15 minutes prior to bedtime and to continue these while he was in bed until he fell asleep. After bedtime was under control, treatment then focused on generalizing relaxation to his stressful workplace and brainstorming ways to reduce the stress at work.

Relaxation 101

Anxiety is often present—and sometimes prominent—in clients attempting to moderate or eliminate problem drinking. One of the coauthors has found that a very good way to help clients learn to control anxiety is by using a particular breathing technique to reduce the physical symptoms of anxiety—shallow breathing, tense muscles, distracting and catastrophic thoughts. The breathing technique, called diaphragmatic breathing, slows down breathing and allows the body to relax. It takes practice, but most clients can master it in a few sessions. *As with any technique like this, it is important for clients to check with their physicians to make certain there are no physical problems that would be compromised by doing this breathing technique. Be sure to tell the client that anxiety can increase at the beginning of learning this technique but that it usually goes away quickly.*

1. Ask the client to sit comfortably upright in a chair with his or her feet on the floor and hands resting comfortably on the arms of the chair or the thighs.

2 Tell the client that he or she can keep eyes open or closed, whichever is more comfortable.

3. Tell the client to begin focusing on his or her breathing, the easy way the air flows in and out, how muscles relax upon exhaling. Tell the client, "Just allow yourself to feel comfortable breathing in . . . and out.

4. Then ask the client to place one hand on his or her upper chest and one hand on his or her diaphragm. Explain that anxious breathing usually causes the upper chest to rise and fall, and that deep, slow, relaxed breathing expands the diaphragm. Ask the client to take in and let out several deep, slow breaths and determine in which part (upper or lower chest) he or she is breathing. Tell the client that breathing that expands the diaphragm takes time to learn and not to be concerned if it isn't happening right away.

5. Next, tell the client that you would like him or her to breathe in very slowly to a count of four or five. (Clients who smoke may only be able to breathe in to a count of three. Reassure them that this is not a problem and that they will progress as they practice more.) Then tell them that they should exhale slowly to a count of four or five. Exhalation can take longer than inhalation, so reassure the client that this is normal.

6. Then ask the client to pause very briefly before taking in the next breath, if possible. If this is not possible, simply reiterate that the breathing should be done very slowly and very comfortably.

7. Practice this type of breathing regularly in session, and ask the client to practice it daily at home. Be sure to tell the client to do this breathing technique while sitting in a chair in a quiet room at home or in a nonstressful, non-trigger-filled environment. Clients are usually able to do at least one session of five slow breaths in less than 10 minutes.

As we said earlier, triggers can be just about anything. As Kathleen Carroll suggests in the chapter entitled "Behavioral and Cognitive Behavioral Techniques" in *Addictions, A Comprehensive Guidebook*, it is important to assess all the aspects of the client's life to determine what his or her triggers are. With whom does the client use? Where? What are the emotional states associated with use? What thoughts accompany the use? ("I can't deal with this unless I've got something to drink." "I deserve to get drunk." "If I don't drink right now, I won't be able to handle it.") Thoughts often predate feelings, and the two together prompt behaviors (drinking).

It is also important to examine the *chain* of triggers that can accompany alcohol use. For example, a client treated by one of the coauthors felt an overwhelming desire to take a drink before work. He said that it made him feel more sociable with his supervisors and coworkers, something that made his shift seem to go faster. His thought was "These guys won't like me if I'm not loose." His habit was to put a flask in the glove compartment of his truck, pull into the parking lot at work, have the equivalent of two to three drinks, and then go in. He accurately noted, however, that he began to want a drink significantly before he pulled into the parking lot. As we backtracked through his chain of triggers, he identified that he began thinking about opening the flask and anticipating taking a drink when he passed a certain street. The desire for a drink escalated as he read other street name signs until finally he was in the parking lot when his craving was at its highest. An intelligent man, he quickly realized that driving by these streets was a powerful trigger for him. During (and after) treatment, he not only decided to take a different route to work, he also swapped vehicles with his wife so that he would not associate the glove compartment in that car with the flask and the drinking. Two years after treatment—and well on his way to recovery—he would change routes whenever he felt he was beginning to think about drinking before work. (He reported that this did not occur often and that he rather enjoyed the change as it kept him from being bored.)

Another client had a similar reaction when she saw an old flame—and drinking buddy—on the streets of her small town. Her triggers also included seeing the street where he lived, any of his family members, and even the wallet whose leather still had an impression of the card on which she had written her old flame's telephone number years before. She quickly decided to get rid of the wallet, but she could not move out of town because she did not want to force her husband to find a new job and her children to attend a new school, as they were doing well and were happy in their current school. Part of her treatment then was to use new cognitions and relaxation techniques to help reduce the impact of the triggers she could not avoid. When she recognized a trigger, she learned to tell herself, "Breathe slowly. This is just a trigger, and I know how to handle it." After a while she became so adept at this that the triggers lost their impact. This client even went to a class reunion at which her old flame was present, and she later proudly reported no impact that she could not handle.

You can see how important it is to take a look at everything in the client's life—from thoughts and feelings to behaviors, as well as people, places, and things—when developing a relapse prevention plan.

Developing a Relapse Prevention Plan

Relapse prevention planning takes place early in treatment. It is not an afterthought. Indeed, it is part and parcel of treatment. The client uses identification of triggers, thoughts, and feelings as a method of identifying goals and maintaining goal orientation during treatment.

It is not unusual for a client to be ambivalent about entering or participating in treatment. Even highly motivated clients have doubts. Part of the work of treatment is helping the client to identify the costs and benefits of changing or maintaining behaviors. A client of one of the coauthor's calls this "getting the whole picture," because it examines behavior change or behavior maintenance from all aspects, even the side that looks at reasons *not* to stop drinking. This is usually very surprising to clients because typically no one—and rarely family members who are not using—has ever asked them before about the benefits of not changing. But if all aspects of the problem are not examined, problem solving and decision making will be difficult if not impossible, and the client often assumes that you are just like everyone else—that is, pushing him or her to get into treatment, get sober, and so on.

For that reason, one of the first things to do in relapse prevention planning is examine the costs and benefits of changing or maintaining behavior. This exercise is written on a piece of paper divided into quadrants and labeled. In each quadrant the client is asked to make a list of the costs or benefits of each of the aspects. This can be time consuming and should not be rushed. It can take place over several sessions if necessary. The client needs time to think about his or her alcohol problems in a new way. A sample of a completed cost-benefit analysis table might look something like the one in Figure 7.1.

When the table is complete, the client is then asked, "What do you notice?" In the case of our sample table, it's pretty clear that the costs of not changing and the benefits of changing outweigh the benefits of not changing and the costs of changing. But the client may not always see this. The client's responses will be very telling about what stage of change (precontemplation, contemplation, or preparation) the client is in. During this process, the therapist may want to use the motivational interviewing techniques discussed earlier in this book to capitalize on the client's own thoughts about his or her problems with alcohol.

The cost-benefit analysis table given in this example is only one tool. There are others. A "decision matrix" designed by Marlatt and Gordon examines immediate positive and negative consequences of drinking behavior, and delayed or long-term positive and negative consequences.

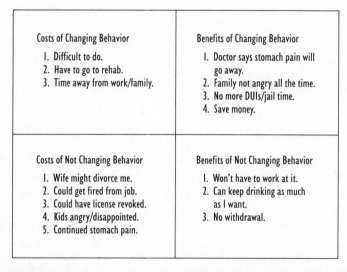

Costs of Changing Behavior	Benefits of Changing Behavior
1. Difficult to do. 2. Have to go to rehab. 3. Time away from work/family.	1. Doctor says stomach pain will go away. 2. Family not angry all the time. 3. No more DUIs/jail time. 4. Save money.
Costs of Not Changing Behavior	Benefits of Not Changing Behavior
1. Wife might divorce me. 2. Could get fired from job. 3. Could have license revoked. 4. Kids angry/disappointed. 5. Continued stomach pain.	1. Won't have to work at it. 2. Can keep drinking as much as I want. 3. No withdrawal.

Figure 7.1: Costs and benefits of changing or maintaining behavior.

Dealing with Cravings and Urges

Cravings, defined as a longing for alcohol, and urges, defined as the intent to do something to satisfy the craving (i.e., take a drink), are usually a part of the treatment mode. As such, they also need to be part of relapse prevention planning. As with any type of addictive behavior, the craving for alcohol and the urge to drink are coupled with thoughts about drinking—thoughts that are rarely negative. Indeed, most clients in early recovery with alcohol problems have positive thoughts about what the outcome of cravings and urges would be. These are known as "positive outcome expectancies." Marlatt writes,

> *These outcome expectancies develop from several potential sources: (a) classical conditioning, in which drug cues serve as conditioned stimuli for a conditioned craving response, (b) exposure to high-risk situations coupled with low self-efficacy for coping, (c) physical dependence or withdrawal, (d) personal and cultural beliefs about expected effects of substance or behavior, and (e) environmental settings where consumption takes place.*

Let's take these one at a time. First, classical conditioning. Remember Pavlov's dogs? They salivated naturally when meat powder was put in their mouths. Later, when a particular tone was paired with the presentation of the meat powder, they *learned* to salivate when they heard the tone. In and of itself, the tone wouldn't have produced salivation, but because it was paired with meat powder, which would naturally have made the dogs salivate, the tone became a stimulus—a trigger—that produced salivation. So how does this work in the case of addictions? Recall the patient who began to crave alcohol when he drove past a certain street sign. The street sign itself would never have made him think of a drink, but because it was paired with the anticipation of alcohol—along with several other stimuli (triggers)—he was conditioned to think of a drink when he drove by it.

Second, exposure to high-risk situations with low ability to cope with them. A good example of this is the client who got off work and was invited to the bar by his buddies. He might not know how to say "no, thanks" without offending them or seeming antisocial. So he says yes, fully intending not to drink but to just have a soda or a cup of coffee. But when they arrive at the bar, his buddies tease and chide him until he has a drink or two or more. This client may well be able to have a drink without risk, but if his goal was abstinence, in his mind he becomes a failure. In this case, the client didn't have the coping skills to deal with the high-risk situation. What are the coping skills he might have used? First, he and the therapist could have identified this as a high-risk situation and role-played ways he could cope with it. He would have decided ahead of time how he wanted to handle the situation and together with the therapist could have selected how he wanted to respond without angering his buddies or feeling like an outcast.

Third, physical dependence or withdrawal. By the time a client has developed dependence, he or she may have experienced several bouts of withdrawal. It is not pleasant, and in the worst-case scenario it can be life threatening. The client then associates not drinking with the unpleasant physical sensations of withdrawal. The thought that usually accompanies this is "I can't stand this." or "I'll die if I have to go through this again." These are potent thoughts. They are also inaccurate thoughts, but they are likely to foster a lapse. The client who is physically dependent on alcohol must be evaluated by a physician knowledgeable about physical dependence and withdrawal. Depending upon the severity, the client may have to undergo medically supervised withdrawal in a hospital or similar facility.

Fourth, many clients are likely to have certain thoughts or beliefs about alcohol that stem from their cultural orientation. These situations can encompass everyone from people whose religion involves ingestion of alcohol to clients whose families have always used alcohol and don't have an understanding of those who have developed alcohol use problems.

Finally, the environmental factor, the "places" of people, places, and things. Environments are powerful triggers. When thinking about environments, the first thing that usually occurs to a client is the place where he or she usually drank: a bar, a country club, a favorite restaurant. However, these are only the most obvious. The clients that one of the coauthors worked with had numerous environments in which they drank. Here are just a few: a picnic area, the car or truck, the family room or basement at home, the deck at home or at a friend's, a park, the area behind a state liquor store or grocery store, a hunting stand or camp, a boat on a lake.

Steps in Creating a Relapse Prevention Plan

Earlier in this chapter, we talked about one of the first steps to creating a relapse prevention plan: a cost-benefit analysis or decision matrix. This makes a good foundation for the rest of the steps.

- First, some ground rules. It is important to remember that relapse prevention planning, like any therapy, has to be collaborative. The client is likely only to give lip service to a plan developed without his or her input, and the chance of failure is very high.
- Second, any relapse prevention plan has to be tested. The client will have to learn the plan, implement the plan, and then determine how successful it was. If there were glitches or potential pitfalls, the plan has to be modified to make it a "custom fit."

There are numerous ways to create a relapse prevention plan. A variety of them are available on the Internet. Others can be found in popular books at bookstores. Still others can be found in textbooks. The relapse prevention plan offered here combines a step-by-step process with cognitive and behavioral guides designed to cover as many aspects of lapse/relapse as possible. While much of the process will be done verbally, *the final product should be written.*

Copies will be given to the client, to designated family members or anyone who will be assisting the client with his or her recovery process, and any therapist who is working with the client.

The steps:

1. Cost-benefit analysis. This exercise not only starts the client thinking about relapse prevention but also underscores and illuminates the gains he or she made in treatment. Additionally, it teaches an important skill that can be generalized to a variety of different contexts.

2. Trigger Identification. As we mentioned, triggers can be just about anything (thoughts, feelings, people, places, things, smells), so it will be important to cover all aspects of a client's life—work, school, family, social settings, behaviors, finances, legal situations, and the related thoughts and feelings—to identify the triggers specific to that client.

3. Thought identification. What is going through the client's mind when he or she is thinking about drinking, thinking about recovery, thinking about relapse? Brainstorm with the client new thoughts that support recovery. These can even be written on 3x5 cards that the client can carry to refer to and connect with.

4. Identification of past events or situations that triggered previous lapses or relapses. In this step, also be sure to note what worked well before to head off a lapse. This is where you and the client will begin to look at his or her "toolbox" of coping skills. What stress reduction tools does he or she have? What about social skills deficits? Self-care? How well is the client taking care of him- or herself?

5. Identification of warning signs. Note that this is plural: warning *signs*. Rarely is there just one. It is important to identify as many as possible. Is a lapse near when the client is angry? Ill? Overreacting? Missing meetings? Missing appointments with a therapist? Feeling lonely? Having job stress? Stress at home?

The final product should have a title (such as "My Personal Relapse Plan" or "Stay Safe Plan," or, as one of the coauthor's clients titled hers, "My Keys to Freedom"). Then there will be categories, such as "Personal Triggers," "Early Warning Signs," "Early Warning Thoughts," "What Helps if I Experience Early Warning Signs," and "Who Do I Want to Help Me and How I Want Them to Help." Under these categories will be the specific things the client and you generated to create the relapse prevention plan.

Monitoring Progress

One of the questions that often comes up from both clinicians and concerned others is "how do I know (client) is telling the truth about his/her drinking?" We touched on this very briefly in the last chapter (and Appendix B expands upon our views in this regard), but this issue arises so often that we want to visit it again before we conclude this chapter on relapse prevention.

The fact of the matter is that, unless you observe the client drinking or he/she comes to your office obviously intoxicated, there is no sure fire way of knowing whether the client is telling the truth about maintaining abstinence or moderation. That being said, there are ways that you as a clinician can minimize the likelihood that a client will be less than truthful about their drinking. In fact, research has shown that, contrary to popular lore (an old treatment provider jokes goes "How do you know an alcoholic is lying? Her lips are moving"), clients are typically quite honest about their drinking if certain conditions are in place. These are:

1. A solid, respectful, and empathetic therapeutic alliance.
2. Clients are assured that reports of drinking to the clinician will not be divulged to others without the client's permission (e.g., basic client-clinician confidentiality applies).
3. Negative sanctions and/or clinician disapproval for truthful reporting are avoided.

Clinicians who establish these conditions greatly increase the likelihood that clients will be truthful with them about alcohol consumption.

Biological monitoring is often thought of as useful in monitoring lapses, or relapse when working with substance users. For alcohol, there is no reliable biological monitoring method other than urine or breath alcohol analysis, and while those are accurate while alcohol remains unmetabolized in the body (about 1 hour for each drink the individual consumes) unlike biological monitoring for other drugs (e.g., marijuana, cocaine, heroin, amphetamines) the "detection window" for alcohol is a matter of hours rather than days. Thus, unless the client has consumed alcohol within a very short time of being asked to submit a biological specimen, it is unlikely that any alcohol will be detected. For this reason, biological monitoring with clients who are attempting to stop drinking is iffy. Clearly, for those whose goal is moderation, it is nearly useless, unless the specimen is taken within a very short time after the last drink is consumed.

Working the Relapse Prevention Plan

Remember the old joke about a tourist in New York asking a cabbie, "How do you get to Carnegie Hall?" The cabbie drolly replied, "Practice, practice, practice."

How does a client get comfortable with the skills he or she is going to need to maintain treatment goals, including the relapse prevention plan? Practice, practice, practice. In the safety of the therapy room, a client can practice role-playing his or her new skills until they feel comfortable and are easily accessible to the client during the time that he or she will most need them.

Finally, remember that a relapse prevention plan, like any plan, may need to be changed or updated. The client will have to spend time testing the plan to see what works and what needs to be fine-tuned or eliminated.

Key Terms

Cognitive Behavior Therapy. Therapy that incorporates addressing dysfunctional thinking as well as behavioral techniques to combat a variety of psychological problems. Albert Ellis and Donald Meichenbaum are generally credited as originators of this empirically validated type of therapy.

Cognitive Therapy. Therapy originated by Aaron Beck and Albert Ellis. Cognitive therapy, which is empirically validated, posits that the way an individual thinks has a significant impact on feelings and behavior, and that dysfunctional thoughts are at the heart of many psychological disorders.

Cue. A signal that can precipitate an action.

Lapse. An initial return to the use of alcohol, or a transgression of one's goal regarding alcohol use.

Relapse. A return to pretreatment status or the problem use of alcohol.

Relapse prevention. A collaboratively derived comprehensive plan for preventing relapse.

Trigger. An event that hastens or brings on a behavior, usually an unwanted behavior.

Recommended Reading

Relapse Prevention: Maintenance in the Treatment of Addictive Behaviors, 2nd Edition, by G. Alan Marlatt (New York: Guilford, 2005).

TRUTH OR FICTION

QUIZ ANSWERS

1. False   2. False   3. True   4. True   5. True

CHAPTER 8

Culture, Coaching, and Change: Moving Beyond Alcohol Problems

TRUTH OR FICTION

QUIZ

After reading this chapter, you will be able to answer true or false to the following statements:

1. Alcohol problems are pretty much the same across ethnic and cultural groups. True or False?

2. When working with members of a particular cultural or ethnic group, you can assume that the patient is pretty much like other members of that group. True or False?

3. The process of overcoming alcohol problems is a lifelong one that demands constant vigilance on the part of the patient for success. True or False?

4. The use of booster sessions after formal treatment has finished can enhance long-term treatment outcome. True or False?

5. Relapse is a common phenomenon following alcohol treatment, but one that can actually be beneficial to the change process. True or False?

Answers on p. 33.

Culture and Ethnicity in Changing Alcohol Problems: Different Strokes for Different Folks

Well, we've come to the last chapter of the book, and although it's been a long journey, we still have some issues to discuss. We want to bring everything together in this chapter and to raise some further issues that we believe are important for clinicians to consider in working with patients seeking to overcome alcohol problems.

The first area we want to write about is the role that patient ethnicity and culture play (or don't play) in the change process. We've left this until last because we believe that ethnicity and culture are general issues that must be acknowledged and addressed specifically with all patients and at all stages of treatment. These issues are often among the most difficult for clinicians to

> "Culture is the widening of the mind and of the spirit."
>
> —JAWAHARLAL NEHRU

address because of potential ethnic and cultural differences between clinician and patient and because some important ethnic and cultural considerations seem so sensitive in our society that clinicians are frequently reluctant to raise them. For example, a Caucasian therapist might experience anxiety asking an African American patient about their experience of prejudice. Nonetheless, addressing these concerns can be a critical factor in determining whether or not a clinician's efforts are successful.

The importance of ethnic and cultural considerations becomes clear when one reads the ethnographic research on the different roles alcohol plays in different cultures, even to the point of how behavior associated with intoxication is both displayed and viewed by the culture itself. These views also play a role in the types of problems associated with heavy drinking and in the acceptability of abstinence versus moderation drinking goals. For example, in France, the distribution of types of alcohol-related problems among native-born French people tends to be skewed toward the development of medical problems rather than the social or criminal problems seen frequently in the United States. In Arabic or Islamic cultures, alcohol use is often forbidden completely, making a moderation goal less acceptable than complete abstinence. In cultures that place a premium on family structure and emphasize respect for elders and a subordination of individual needs and desires for the good of the family, treatments that emphasize personal autonomy and independence may not be as well received as treatments emphasizing compliance and rule-following. We could continue this list of examples almost endlessly, but you get the sense how important ethnic and cultural issues can be in working with a particular patient.

However, we urge clinicians to approach ethnic and cultural issues carefully and with the same individualized attitude we have urged clinicians to take with respect to alcohol problems themselves. This means that the clinician should not assume that because a patient comes from a particular ethnic or cultural background, he or she strongly identifies with that background. Straussner (2003) cautions that even in so-called "tightly knit" cultures, particular individuals may vary in the degree to which they or their families identify with that culture's values. The only way to gauge the depth and importance of a patient's ethnic and cultural background is to ask the patient about it.

A variety of factors influence the degree to which a patient identifies with his or her ethnic or cultural background, and by implication the importance that working within the mores and customs of that background may influence the outcome of treatment. A number of these factors are presented in Table 8.1. They include the relative generational gap between the family's arrival in their country of residence and the patient's birth. Third-generation family members often do not identify as strongly with their immigrant ancestors' cultural values

Table 8.1: Sample Questions for Assessing Ethnic Identity.

1. With what ethnic/cultural or religious group would you say you most closely identify?
2. Are you proud to be a(n) (client's asserted ethnic group)?
3. If you could be reborn into any ethnic group of your choosing, would you choose to be reborn as a(n) (client's asserted ethnic group)?
4. Have you ever been the victim of discrimination or prejudice because you are a member of (ethnic group)? If yes, how did you react to that?
5. To what extent do you make it a point to participate in activities that are strongly associated with your ethnic group (e.g., group political activities, religious festivals, community organizations)?
6. Do you speak the language of your ethnic group? If yes, do you speak it at home instead of speaking English?

as do children who were born abroad but were brought to their country of residence as babies or were born shortly after arrival. Patients who immigrate as teens or young adults may find themselves caught between cultures. On the one hand, they want to be part of the culture of their peers, while feeling pressure to maintain the customs and mores of the parents' country of origin. The only way to know this is to assess it.

Assessing the degree to which ethnicity and culture may influence the course of treatment requires a direct, open, and empathetic line of questioning by the clinician. Some suggested opening questions are presented in Table 8.1. It is important that the clinician also be aware of his or her own reactions to members of particular ethnic or cultural groups. To use but one of many possible examples, a therapist who identifies herself as Jewish may have difficulty both understanding and assessing a patient who is Muslim from a Palestinian family. As with other aspects of ethnicity and culture, the degree to which these sorts of differences will influence a clinician's ability to relate to, understand, and assist a patient will vary from clinician to clinician. Clinicians need to be aware of how their own ethnic and cultural backgrounds influence not only their views of the nature of alcohol problems and their resolution but also how they react to patients of various ethnic or cultural backgrounds. While none of us like to think of ourselves as prejudiced we often absorb subtle messages from our own culture and ethnic background that may not be influential in our interactions with others until we meet a patient of a particular ethnic or cultural background.

Another issue that it is important to recognize within the scope of ethnicity and culture is how the patient's ethnic or cultural group views alcohol problems. For instance, among people who were not born and raised in the U.S. the notion that alcohol problems stem from a "disease" may be an unfamiliar concept to people from a particular ethnic or cultural background. Many cultures view problems with alcohol as a moral failing or a failure of willpower, rather than as the result of a disease. For patients who identify strongly with an ethnic or cultural group that holds such a view, treatment that emphasizes the disease concept (as do the vast majority of formal treatments in the United States) may be difficult to grasp and internalize. Likewise, for a patient from a non-Christian religious background, the notion of spirituality and the decidedly Judeo-Christian tone of much of the 12-step philosophy that drives most U.S. treatment may be difficult to understand and accept.

The diversity and sheer number of ethnic and cultural considerations that patients may bring to treatment makes a thorough discussion in this chapter impossible. There are a number of useful resources for clinicians to seek out when attempting to help a patient from an ethnic or cultural background with which the clinician is not familiar. Straussner's (2003) edited volume listed in the suggested readings at the end of the book is a useful starting point. We want to leave the reader with this advice about working with patients whose ethnic or cultural background differs from yours: As part of your initial assessment, ask about the patient's ethnic or cultural identification and how important it is to him or her, and then work within the patient's self-assessment. Do not base treatment only on appearances (a person appearing to be of Asian or African-American ethnicity may not identify strongly with either set of ethnic or cultural customs and mores), but don't be afraid to ask about cultural or ethnic factors.

Defining and Maintaining a Healthy Lifestyle

For most clinicians, the ultimate goal of any alcohol-focused intervention is to assist the client in moving toward a healthier, more fulfilling lifestyle. It is important to recognize, however, that this may *not* be the client's ultimate goal. Client goals for themselves and consequently what the client will consider a successful, healthy outcome may differ from the clinician's notions of those very same concepts. The bottom line is that, as with virtually every aspect of working with clients who have problems with alcohol, it can be both presumptuous and hazardous to treatment for a clinician to decide that he or she knows what the client wants to achieve.

There is no universal definition of "health" that would be accepted as a worthy goal by all individuals with alcohol-related problems. For some clients, simply reducing the direct negative effects of over-drinking (hangovers the next day, for example, or missing too many days from work recovering from hangovers) may be enough for the client to believe that he or she has achieved significant positive strides toward health. For another client, the definition of health may include improved interpersonal relationships or repairing ones that have been damaged as a result of the client's drinking. Depending on the client's financial circumstances, a healthy work life might include being able to physically accomplish tasks involving heavy labor that were a big part of the client's vocational life before drinking became a problem. For yet another client, vocational health may mean being more creative and mentally sharp at work.

> "It is good to have an end to journey toward, but it is the journey that matters in the end."
>
> —URSULA K. LE GUIN

These simple examples of the extraordinary level of diversity among clients in terms of ethnocultural factors and personal views of what is desirable in life again brings us back to our primary focus in virtually everything we have written: Ask the client what the desired outcome is rather than assuming that we as clinicians have some objective touchstone for defining health. As with all other aspects of intervention we have discussed, this means doing a specific assessment with each patient of his or her views of what it means to be healthy in a variety of life domains (work/school, family, physical health, social interactions, recreation, etc.) and how important it is to the patient's personal sense of well-being that a particular life domain be marked by a high degree of healthiness (see Table 8.2).

Table 8.2: Lifestyle Domains.

Family
Social
Work/Educational
Health/Diet/Fitness
Recreational
Spiritual/Religious

In a sense, helping a client to generate a personal definition of "health" is very much a motivational exercise. As discussed in a previous chapter, lasting behavior change happens most readily when several factors are present in a person's life. These include (1) a sense of personal autonomy or agency in life—that one is the ultimate decision-maker with respect to important goals and lifestyle issues, (2) a supportive environment that does not stand in the way of achieving the individual's personal goals, (3) a sense of personal efficacy—that one can, by one's efforts, achieve at least part of the goals one sets for oneself, and (4) a sense that what one is working toward is important and worth striving for. When these factors are in place, and a client has the requisite skills to achieve one's primary (e.g., personally most important) goals, lasting behavior changes become much more likely. People change most reliably when they are moving *toward* a life that they perceive as better than the one they are trying to avoid or the one about which they are, at best, ambivalent.

In order to help clients define a healthy outcome and lifestyle after intervention, we suggest using the same client-focused and individualized approaches that we wrote about in earlier chapters on interventions. These include Scaling and Decisional Balance exercises that can help clients define what a healthy lifestyle might be for themselves.

The process of using Scaling and Decisional Balance exercises to assist in defining healthy lifestyle outcomes is essentially the same as the process of defining viable use goals and motivation. Asking the client to rate the importance of various lifestyle domains for their personal sense of well-being on a zero to 10 scale and then asking the client to define which aspects of a particular domain are most important is the first step in the process of defining a healthy outcome. The process becomes a highly interactive one when the client rates a lifestyle domain quite low (e.g., a young person who rates improved physical health as less important than, say having many friends), seemingly ignoring potential risks associated with alcohol use for achieving health in that domain. When this happens, the clinician can ask the client the scaling questions we discussed in an earlier chapter. Such a dialogue might look something like this:

T: You've given Physical Health a rating of "5" on importance for you at this time. It seems that maintaining physical health is not a high priority for you right now. Is that an accurate assessment on my part?

C: Yeah, I'm pretty healthy right now, and all those medical problems we talked about that could happen if I continued to drink like I was when I started treatment, well, those aren't going to happen now because I've cut down a lot on my drinking.

T: That's true, and I hope you're as pleased about the changes in your drinking as I am. However, I want to explore the importance of keeping physically healthy a bit more. Are you willing?

C: Sure, what did you have in mind?

T: I'm wondering what would have to happen or change in your life to make keeping physically healthy more important to you? What would it take for your rating of "5" to move to, let's say, a "7"?

C: Well, I guess I'd have to actually have some of the GI or other problems we talked about before.

T: So, since you're not actually sick now, it seems less important to you to focus energy on maintaining your health.

C: Yeah, I have lots of other things I'd rather do.

T: I think it's interesting though, that you didn't rate yourself a "2" on the importance of maintaining your health. Why a "5" and not a "2"?

C: I'd be stupid to say that my health isn't important at all to me, it's just that it's not the highest priority in my life right now.

T: Would you be willing to take a closer look at the importance of maintaining physical health by doing a Decisional Balance sheet with me? I'd like us to examine the pros and cons of maintaining a physically healthy lifestyle— eating well, exercising, and, of course, maintaining your drinking at its current, safe level. What do you say?

At this point, the therapist and client might complete a Decisional Balance sheet focusing on the pros and cons of making health-promoting behaviors a priority versus waiting until the client's health begins to worsen before focusing on health behaviors.

As with other motivational interventions, the therapist can provide objective information about the benefits to maintaining safer drinking levels and one's physical health (e.g., exercise and other health-related behaviors are known to relieve stress, help with sleeping, etc.) and suggest and explore possible ways to do so easily and with less effort than the client may anticipate will be required. As with the work at the beginning of treatment on client motivation to change, this discussion will ultimately aim to raise the client's consciousness of the importance of this life domain for maintaining changes in drinking, help the client brainstorm viable ways of achieving a healthier lifestyle given the client's current life situation, and assist the client in taking action to enhance well-being in this life domain.

This is a very individualized and client-centered approach. As such, it is important for the clinician to be aware of and address his or her own counter-transference issues when the client assigns a high level of importance to behaviors that the clinician finds personally objectionable or believes will be detrimental to the client. For example, a client may insist that changing his/her diet from nearly constant fast food to a more balanced diet that adheres more closely to nutritional guidelines is not important. Or a client may plan to use other drugs besides alcohol or continue to smoke cigarettes that the clinician believes the client should avoid because of the personal and social risk involved. The clinician's role in such cases is to provide objective, non-judgmental information and feedback to the client, attempt to help the client shift perspective, but if the client does not shift, then accept the client's view, at least for the moment, and move on. As with changes in drinking behavior, it is critical that the therapist not engage in unwanted directiveness, paternalism, or "expertism" with the client. Instead, the therapist should be a sounding board who can be trusted to listen to the client's concerns and not belittle them as impractical.

Summing Up

We've come to the end of our journey toward an evidence-based, client-centered approach to working with clients with alcohol problems. Throughout this book we have attempted to keep the focus squarely where it belongs—on the client. We've written over and over about individualized assessments, individualized applications of change methodologies, and supporting autonomous client decisions about changing drinking behavior. It is our belief, which we hope you now share, that this approach (which harkens back to the early days of AA) is consistent with the best research into how people successfully change their problems with alcohol. And it is an approach that allows clinicians to be collaborators with their clients rather than parents to them!

We'd like to leave you with a few reminders about the basics of this approach and hope that you will try it with the next client who comes to you for help with alcohol-related problems. We think you'll be pleased with how much easier your work becomes and how much more responsive the client is to the process of change.

THINGS TO REMEMBER

1. One size does not fit all in resolving alcohol problems. It requires "different strokes for different folks." Customization is the key to success.

2. Approaching clients in an empathetic, respectful, and collaborative manner that is nonprescriptive will lead clients to become more rapidly engaged and persistent in their efforts to change their drinking.

3. Clients are in charge of their decisions and make their own choices. Clinicians only coach from the sidelines.

4. Good coaches coach to strengthen rather than focusing on their weakness. Make use of your client's strengths in helping them develop a workable change plan.

5. Assessment and feedback of assessment data at every stage of change are critical to helping clients define an effective change strategy for themselves.

6. Change is generally gradual; effective clinicians reinforce and affirm even small changes their clients make that move them toward a healthier life.

7. It's important for clinicians to be attuned to their own biases and counter-transference toward clients and to attempt to either overcome them or refer the client to another clinician.

As with clients, we believe that clinicians also decide how they will approach and work with clients. We hope that we have tipped your decisional balance toward a more empathetic and collaborative way of working with clients that help them take charge of their own recovery from problems with alcohol, no matter how big those problems are!

Key Terms

Cultural/ethnic identification. The degree to which an individual actually identifies himself or herself as a member of the cultural or ethnic group to which his or her parents belong. This is highly variable from individual to individual, and must be specifically assessed for each client.

Healthy lifestyle. Critical to sustaining changes in drinking over time, but an elusive concept that is often idiosyncratic to a particular client. As with cultural and ethnic identity, a healthy lifestyle must be specifically assessed with each client. While general notions of health (e.g., low fat diet, exercise, absence of medical problems) are useful, each client may have his or her own views of what is healthy and how important a healthy lifestyle is to him or her.

"Expertism." Relationship style in which the clinician acts as an "expert" who knows what is best for the client, and makes prescriptions for the client to follow based on the clinician's ideas of what is best. This stance is often fatal to effective treatment of clients with alcohol problems, and should be avoided unless the client asks the clinician for his or her expert opinion.

Recommended Reading

Practicing Harm Reduction Psychotherapy: An Alternative Approach to Addictions, by P. Denning (New York: Guilford, 2000).

"Ethnic Identity in Adolescents and Adults: Review of Research," by J. S. Phinney (1990), in *Psychological Bulletin, 108,* pp. 499–514.

Ethnocultural Factors in Substance Abuse Treatment, edited by S. L. A. Straussner (New York: Guilford, 2001).

Counseling the Culturally Different: Theory and Practice, 3rd Edition, by D. W. Sue and D. Sue (New York: Wiley, 1999).

TRUTH OR FICTION

QUIZ ANSWERS

1. False   2. False   3. False   4. True   5. True

APPENDIX A

Locating and Selecting Treatment Programs for Referrals

There are a number of ways clinicians can go about selecting potential specialty programs to which to refer clients with alcohol problems. Some have been discussed earlier in the book and involve doing local canvassing of phone books, other treatment providers, etc. However, this is not always an effective or efficient way of identifying programs, particularly if your client is resistant to the dominant 12-step approach taken by most treatment programs or has moderation rather than abstinence as the treatment goal. Ads appearing in phone books or newspapers are not always obvious about the program's philosophy and approach. In order to provide the best possible referral for a client, it helps to have a variety of questions in mind to ask programs or providers to whom you are thinking of making a referral.

Joseph Volpicelli and Maia Szalavitz in their book *Recovery Options: The Complete Guide* (2000) delineate a number of criteria for clients to use in selecting a treatment program. These are shown in the shaded box on p. 136. Asking these questions before referring clients can make the process of matching the referral to the client's needs much more effective.

It is also important to follow up on the treatment provider's assertions of effectiveness. Asking for specific outcomes (e.g., "How many clients maintain continuous abstinence for a year following your program?" "How many clients resume drinking, but without symptoms, after your program?" "What percentage of clients who start your program complete it?") will give you a pretty good idea of the program's effectiveness in producing changes and whether clients who start the program are likely to finish it. The latter speaks to efforts the program may or may not make to engage and retain clients in treatment. If a program's retention and completion rates are low, this should raise the suspicion that the program is confrontational and, perhaps, insensitive to client needs.

Questions to Ask Potential Referral Resources

1. Is your program (or are you) licensed to provide alcohol treatment services in the state where you are located?

2. What is your program's treatment philosophy? Do you use evidence-based treatments and, if so, which ones?

3. Does your program provide access to or encourage clients to try out non-12-step support groups?

4. Do you have outcome data, specifically retention, completion, and follow-up outcomes for your clients? What are they?

5. What is your program's view regarding the use of medications (1) to treat alcohol problems specifically and (2) to treat co-occurring psychiatric disorders?

6. How do clients resolve problems or issues or complaints?

7. Does your program provide specific informed consent for treatment, and do you have a patient's bill of rights?

8. Is your program HIPAA compliant?

9. Does your program make special provisions for women, gender identity differences, and racial or ethnic background?

10. What is your program's policy regarding family involvement in treatment?

Source: Adapted and expanded from Volpicelli and Szalavitz, 2000.

When you ask these questions you should look for answers that indicate that the program exceeds what has come to be a baseline expectation of program success: That about two-thirds of clients finishing abstinence-focused programs will have resumed drinking at some level within 6–12 months of program completion. This doesn't sound like resounding success, but many programs can legitimately claim better results. For example, a few years ago, the Director of Research at the Hazelden Foundation, one of the best known substance abuse treatment programs in the United States spoke about the results of a survey of clients conducted one year after discharge. It found that 55% of the clients had maintained continuous abstinence for the year, while another 20–25% had resumed use of their substance of choice without *DSM-IV* symptoms of substance use disorder. These are pretty good results with 75–80% of program graduates maintaining gains after a year.

Most programs don't do formal outcome research, so it may be difficult to obtain this information. Programs that are able to provide this information are more likely, in our view, to be using evidence-based approaches to treatment as well.

Specific Resources

A number of resources can be useful in locating treatment programs for clients. The most comprehensive of these is the Substance Abuse and Mental Health Services Administration's (SAMHSA) Treatment Locator available online at http://findtreatment.samhsa.gov/. This is the most comprehensive listing of treatment programs currently available for the United States and includes programs that treat clients with both alcohol and other drug problems. Utilizing a ZIP code search, the website pulls up the names, addresses, contact information and other useful information (e.g., special populations served, inpatient vs. outpatient services) for programs within a certain geographic radius of that ZIP code. Unfortunately, this search engine does not provide information on whether or not non-abstinence goals are permitted for clients, nor does it provide specific information about whether or not the program is strongly focused on 12-step philosophies or not. So, for clients who are looking for alternatives to traditional treatments, you may need to look elsewhere.

Two resources are currently available online that list programs and individual providers that are non-12 step in focus and/or work with clients towards moderation goals. The first is an online book by Melanie Solomon, a recovered alcohol and drug user who has compiled a listing of alternatives to 12-step programs on her website called www.aanottheonlyway.com. The book contains a listing of a number of non-12 step programs and providers around the United States and is available through the website for a cost of $3.95.

Moderation Management (MM) is the support group for people who wish to reduce their drinking (either through abstinence or moderation) to safe levels. MM has a link to a listing of "moderation friendly therapists" on their website at www.moderation.org. This is a free listing and is updated periodically, as is the SAMHSA Treatment Locator.

Finally, to find the most up-to-date information for providers who may not have made the deadlines for recent revisions of these resources, a web search using Google (www.google.com) will often turn up useful referral information.

Unfortunately, the process of finding a good program match for clients is not always an easy one. However, with a bit of legwork it is possible to locate specialty treatment for virtually any client. We hope these few resources will serve as a good starting point for your efforts in this regard.

Reference

Volpicelli, J., & Szalavitz, M. (2000). *Recovery options: The complete guide.* New York: Wiley.

Biological Monitoring and Effective Treatment

In the United States there is a strong movement toward monitoring client recovery through the use of biological monitoring methods such as breath and urine analysis. Because this is such a strong idea—and makes superficial sense to many people who are concerned about their loved ones, employees, or criminal justice clients in their charge—we want to take a few pages to present the facts, as well as our views about biological monitoring of clients with alcohol problems.

First, it is important to recognize that, unlike other drugs that people abuse, alcohol is very rapidly metabolized from the body. The average person eliminates the equivalent of a standard drink in about an hour. Thus, if a person consumes four drinks over the course of four hours, by the end of approximately five hours, all of the alcohol will be gone from that person's body. Of course, there are individual differences in how fast alcohol is eliminated, but it is a fact that alcohol is completely gone from the body within hours of even heavy drinking.

What does this mean for biological monitoring? First, it means that unless the biological specimen (breath, urine, or blood) is taken very shortly after drinking stops (at a time when, if the person has consumed a large amount of alcohol, he or she will likely show behavioral signs that obviate the need for biological samples) biological analyses aiming at detecting alcohol use will always show no use! In fact, for detecting alcohol use, biological monitoring is essentially useless. It is certainly no more effective than behavioral observation unless the behavioral observation is done hours and hours after an extraordinarily heavy bout of drinking when the behavioral disruption of the alcohol may be less that at the beginning of drinking (the descending blood alcohol curve vs. the ascending blood alcohol curve).

So, biological monitoring for the presence of alcohol as a way of determining whether a client or loved one has relapsed is useless. Are there other biological methods that might be used? Researchers have been searching for years for a reliable, nonalcohol biological marker that can detect heavy drinking, but none has ever been shown to be reliable across all drinkers. Patients being treated with medications such as disulfiram or naltrexone can have the administration of the medication monitored through direct observation (as in the Community Reinforcement Approach) or through blood assays that can detect the presence of the medications in the blood. There is no guarantee, however that these medications have, in fact, prevented drinking from occurring.

When examined from a purely biological detection perspective, breath, urine and blood analysis provide no useful way of determining if a person is drinking or not. Nor can other nonalcohol focused assays, such as liver enzyme tests or tests for other biological markers, reliably detect drinking. So, from that perspective alone, biological monitoring is something that clinicians and others should probably avoid.

There is another reason to avoid biological monitoring of clients: the negative reactions many clients have to such monitoring, especially if it is imposed upon them against their wishes. Given our repeated and extensive emphasis on the therapeutic relationship, on respecting and enhancing client autonomy, and on respecting the client as a human being, imposing any measure without the client's active involvement, approval and participation threatens treatment outcome. Imposing biological monitoring without client participation essentially says to the client "I can't trust you."

Well, isn't that a problem with alcohol users generally, that you can't trust them to tell the truth about their drinking? Doesn't the old joke "how do you know an alcoholic is lying? His lips are moving!" hold some truth? In fact, research suggests that the answer to this question is an emphatic "No!" In fact, when a problem drinking client has a solid working alliance with a clinician, is guaranteed confidentiality of information, and faces no punishment for acknowledging drinking, he or she will likely be extremely honest about his or her drinking. The problem comes when others (or, unfortunately, the clinician) attempt to use instances of drinking to prove to the client that he or she cannot manage to alter his or her drinking and sends the message to the client that drinking represents a failure. In the chapter on Relapse Prevention we have discussed the potential toxicity of such a stance by the clinician and others in the client's life. Such situations often evoke anger and resistance from clients and are disruptive to the therapeutic relationship, without which the clinician is doomed to be ineffective in helping clients move toward healthier lives.

Given the lack of any scientific reason for thinking that biological monitoring is more effective than astute behavioral observations as we have outlined above, the potential damage from enforced biological monitoring, in our view, far outweighs any potential gains. We recommend that it *never* be used unless the client (and sometimes clients do) asks for it specifically as a way of helping to achieve the client's personal goals with respect to drinking. If you as a clinician have done your job effectively in establishing a strong therapeutic relationship with your client, biological monitoring will not be necessary because your client will tell you if he or she has exceeded drinking levels that have been agreed upon as therapeutic goals.

REFERENCES

This list includes not only articles and books cited in the text, but a number of other resources that clinicians may find helpful that were not discussed specifically in the text.

Alcoholics Anonymous. Retrieved July 4, 2005 from http://aa.org/default/en_about_aa_sub.cfm?subpageid=14&pageid=24

American Psychiatric Association. (2000). *Diagnostic and statistical manual of mental disorders* (4th ed., text revision). Washington, DC: Author.

American Society of Addiction Medicine. Retrieved July 4, 2005 from http://www.asam.org/search/search2old.html

Brick, J. (Ed.). (2004). *Handbook of the medical consequences of alcohol and drug abuse.* New York: Haworth Press.

Brown, S., Lewis, V. M., & Liotta, A. (2000). *The family recovery guide: A map for healthy growth.* Oakland, CA: New Harbinger.

Blondell, R. (1999). Alcohol abuse and self-neglect in the elderly. *Journal of Elder Abuse and Neglect, 11*(2), 55–75.

Carroll, K.M. (1999). Behavioral and cognitive behavioral treatments. In B. S. McCrady & E. E. Epstein (Eds.), *Addictions: A comprehensive guidebook.* New York: Oxford University Press.

Davis, B. A. (2004). *Development and validation of a scale of perceived control across multiple domains.* Unpublished doctoral dissertation, Philadelphia College of Osteopathic Medicine.

Denning, P. (2000). *Practicing harm reduction psychotherapy: An alternative approach to addictions.* New York: Guilford.

Denning, P., Little, J., & Glickman, A. (2004). *Over the influence: The harm reduction guide for managing drugs and alcohol.* New York: Guilford.

DiClemente, C. C. (2003). *Addiction and change: How addictions develop and addicted people recover.* New York: Guilford.

Donovan, D. M. (1999). Assessment strategies and measures in addictive behaviors. In B. S. McCrady & E. E. Epstein (Eds.), *Addictions: A comprehensive guidebook.* New York: Oxford University Press.

Drake, R. & Mueser, K.T. (2002). Co-occurring alcohol use and schizophrenia. *Alcohol Research and Health.* Retrieved July 4, 2005 from http://www.find articles.com/p/articles/mi_m0CXH/is_2_26/ai_95148610

Eisenberg, A., Eisenberg, H., & Mooney, A. J. (1992). *The recovery book.* New York: Workman.

Finney, J. W., Moos, R. H., & Timko, C. (1999). The course of treated and untreated substance use disorders: Remission and resolution, relapse, and mortality. In B. S. McCrady & E. E. Epstein (Eds.), *Addictions: A comprehensive guidebook.* New York: Oxford University Press.

Fletcher, A.M. (2001). *Sober for good: New solutions for drinking problems— Advice from those who have succeeded.* Boston: Houghton-Mifflin.

Granfield, R., & Cloud, W. (1999). *Coming clean: Overcoming addiction without treatment.* New York: New York University Press.

Grant, B. F. ,& Dawson, D. A. (1999). Alcohol and drug use, abuse, and dependence: Classification, prevalence and comorbidity. In B. S. McCrady & E. E. Epstein (Eds.), *Addictions: A comprehensive guidebook.* New York: Oxford University Press.

Hester, R. K., & Miller, W. R. (Eds.). (2003). *Handbook of alcoholism treatment approaches: Effective alternatives* (3rd ed.). Boston: Allyn & Bacon.

Institute of Medicine. (1990). *Broadening the base of treatment for alcohol problems.* Washington, DC: National Academy Press.

Jongsma, A., & Perkinson, R. (2001). *The addiction treatment planner* (2nd ed.). New York: Wiley.

Klingemann, H., Sobell, L., Barker, J., Blomqvist, J., Cloud, W., Ellinstad, T., Finfgeld, D., Granfield, R., Hodgings, D., Hunt. G., Junker, C., Moggi, F., Peele, S., Smart, R., Sobell, M., & Tucjer, J. (2001). *Promoting self-change from problem substance use: Practical implications for policy, prevention and treatment.* Dordrecht: Kluwer Academic.

Leonard, K. E., & Blane, H. T. (1999). *Psychological theories of drinking and alcoholism* (2nd ed.). New York: Guilford.

Lukas, S. (1993). *Where to start and what to ask: An assessment handbook.* New York: W. W. Norton

McCrady, B. S. (2001). Alcohol use disorders. In D. H. Barlow (Ed.), *Clinical handbook of psychological disorders* (3rd ed., pp. 376–433). New York: Guilford.

McGoldrick, M., Gerson, R., & Shellenberger, S. (1999). *Genograms, assessment and intervention* (2nd ed.). New York: W. W. Norton

Marlatt, G. A. (2005). *Relapse prevention: Maintenance strategies in the treatment of addictive behaviors* (2nd ed.). New York: Guilford.

Marlatt, G. A., & Gordon, J. R. (1985). *Relapse prevention: Maintenance strategies in the treatment of addictive behaviors.* New York: Guilford.

Mayfield, D., McLeod, G., & Hall, P. (1974). The CAGE questionnaire: Validation of a new alcoholism instrument. *American Journal of Psychiatry, 131,* 1121–1123.

Meyers, R. J., & Smith, J. E. (1995). *Clinical guide to alcohol treatment: The community reinforcement approach.* New York: Guilford.

Meyers, R. J., & Wolfe, B. L. (2004). *Get your loved one sober: Alternatives to nagging, pleading and threatening.* Center City, MN: Hazelden.

Milam, J. R., & Ketcham, K. (1984). *Under the influence: A guide to the myths and realities of alcoholism.* New York: Bantam.

Miller, W., & Rollnick, S. (2002). *Motivational interviewing: Preparing people for change.* New York: Guilford.

Miller W., & Rollnick, S. (1991). *Motivational interviewing: Preparing people to change addictive behavior.* New York: Guilford.

Miller, W. R. (1985). Motivation for treatment: A review with special emphasis on alcoholism. *Psychological Bulletin, 98,* 84–107.

Miller, W. R., & Munoz, R. F. (2005). *Controlling your drinking: Tools to make moderation work for you.* New York: Guilford.

Monti, P. M., Kadden, R. M., Rohsenow, D. J., Cooney, N. L., & Abrams, D. B. (2002). *Treating alcohol dependence: A coping skills training manual* (2nd ed.). New York: Guilford.

Morrison, J. (1997). *When psychological problems mask medical disorders: A guide for psychotherapists.* New York: Guilford.

O'Farrell, T. J., & Fals-Stewart, W. (2002). Marital and family therapy in treatment of alcoholism. In D. H. Sprenkel (Ed.), *Effectiveness research in marriage and family therapy* (pp. 123–161). Alexandria, VA: American Association for Marriage and Family Therapy.

Patterson, J., Williams, L., Grauf-Grounds, C., & Chamow, L. (1998). *Essential skills in family therapy, from the first interview to termination.* New York: Guilford.

Phinney, J. S. (1990). Ethnic identity in adolescents and adults: Review of research. *Psychological Bulletin, 108,* 499–514.

Prochaska, J. O., DiClemente, C., & Norcross, J. (1992). In search of how people change: Applications to addictive behaviors. *American Psychologist, 47,* 1102–1114.

Prochaska, J. O., Norcross, J., & DiClemente, C. (1994). *Changing for good, A revolutionary six-stage program for overcoming bad habits and moving your life positively forward.* New York: Avon.

Project MATCH: Series of 8 Manuals. Available from http://www.niaaa.nih.gov/publications/match.htm

Quigley, L. A., & Marlatt, G. A. (1999). Relapse prevention: Maintenance of change after initial treatment. In B. S. McCrady & E. E. Epstein (Eds.), *Addictions: A comprehensive guidebook.* New York: Oxford University Press.

Robins, L. N., Locke, B. Z., & Regier, D. A. (1991). An overview of psychiatric disorders in America. In L. N. Robins & D. A. Regier (Eds.), *Psychiatric disorders in America: The epidemiologic catchment areas study* (pp. 328–366). New York: Free Press.

Rollnick, S., Mason, P., & Butler, C. (1999). *Health behavior change: A guide for practitioners.* New York: Churchill Livingstone.

Rotgers, F., Kern, M. F., & Hoeltzel, R. (2002). *Responsible drinking: A MODERATION MANAGEMENT approach for problem drinkers.* Oakland, CA: New Harbinger.

Rotgers, F., Morgenstern, J., & Walters, S. T. (2003). *Treating substance abuse: Theory and technique* (2nd ed.). New York: Guilford.

Ryan, R. M., & Deci, E. L. (2000). Self-determination theory and the facilitation of intrinsic motivation, social development, and well-being. *American Psychologist, 55,* 68–78.

Sanchez-Craig, M. (1997). *DrinkWise: How to quit drinking or cut down. A self-help book.* Toronto, Canada: Addiction Research Foundation.

Sanjuan, P. M., & Langenbucher, J. W. (1999). Age-limited populations: Youth, adolescents, and older adults. In B. S. McCrady & E. E. Epstein (Eds.), *Addictions: A comprehensive guidebook.* New York: Oxford University Press.

Schuckit, M. A. (1995). *Drug and alcohol abuse: A clinical guide to diagnosis and treatment* (4th ed.). New York: Plenum.

Straussner, S. L. A. (Ed.). (2001). *Ethnocultural factors in substance abuse treatment.* New York: Guilford.

Sue, D. W., & Sue. D. (1999). *Counseling the culturally different: Theory and practice* (3rd ed.). New York: Wiley.

Vaillant, G. E. (1995). *The natural history of alcoholism revisited.* Cambridge, MA: Harvard University Press.

Volpicelli, J. R., Pettinati, H. M., McLellan, A. T., & O'Brien, C. P. (2001). *Combining medication and psychosocial treatments for addictions: The BRENDA approach.* New York: Guilford.

White, W. L. (1998). *Slaying the dragon: The history of addiction treatment and recovery in America.* Bloomington, IL: Chestnut Health Systems.

Workgroup on Substance Abuse Self-Help Groups. (2004). Self help groups for alcohol and drug problems: Toward evidence-based practice and policy. *Journal of Substance Abuse Treatment, 26,* 151–158.

Zinberg, N. E. (1984). *Drug, set, and setting: The basis for controlled intoxicant use.* New Haven: Yale University Press.

INDEX